CoRT THINKING

TEACHER'S NOTES

BREADTH

EDWARD DE BONO

Director. The Cognitive Research Trust (CoRT)

PERGAMON PRESS

NEW YORK · OXFORD · BEIJING · FRANKFURT · SÃO PAULO · SYDNEY · TOKYO · TORONTO

Pergamon Press Offices:

U.S.A.	Pergamon Press, Maxwell House, Fairview Park, Elmsford, New York 10523, U.S.A.
U.K.	Pergamon Press, Headington Hill Hall, Oxford OX3 0BW, ENGLAND
PEOPLE'S REPUBLIC OF CHINA	Pergamon Press, Qianmen Hotel, Beijing, People's Republic of China
FEDERAL REPUBLIC OF GERMANY	Pergamon Press, Hammerweg 6, D-6242 Kronberg, Federal Republic of Germany
BRAZIL	Pergamon Editora, Rua Eca de Queiros, 346 – Paraiso, CEP 04011, São Paulo, Brazil
AUSTRALIA	Pergamon Press (Aust.) Pty., P.O. Box 544, Potts Point, NSW 2011, Australia
JAPAN	Pergamon Press, 8th Floor, Matsuoka Central Building, 1-7-1 Nishishinjuku, Shinjuku-ku, Tokyo 160, Japan
CANADA	Pergamon Press Canada, Suite 104, 150 Consumers Road, Willowdale, Ontario M2J 1P9, Canada

First Edition 1973

Reprinted 1981 Pergamon Press Limited
Second Edition 1986

ISBN 0–08 027421 8

Designed, printed and bound in Great Britain
by A. Wheaton & Co. Ltd., Exeter.

CONTENTS

BACKGROUND TO THE TEACHING OF THINKING

FOREWORD

The **CoRT** Thinking Lessons are now the most widely used materials for the direct teaching of thinking as a basic skill. The lessons have been in use since 1970 and in the intervening years a great deal of experience in the direct teaching of thinking as a skill has been accumulated. I write this because it is not difficult to devise new programs which seem exciting at first but which do not withstand the test of time and use. Excitement and novelty are no substitute for practicality and experience.

The **CoRT** Thinking Lessons, in six sections, are now in heavy use throughout the U.S.A., in the U.K., Ireland, Canada, Australia, New Zealand, Israel and Malta. In Venezuela, after a year's pilot program, the **CoRT** Thinking Lessons have been added on to the curriculum of every school in the country. A number of other countries have already expressed interest in following this example.

The success of the **CoRT** Thinking Lessons has depended on two things: an increasing interest in the teaching of thinking as a basic skill and the practical, hands-on nature of the lessons.

There is a growing feeling amongst educators that thinking is a skill that should be given direct attention. It is felt that thinking is a skill that can be improved by focused attention and the practice of some basic skills. The old idea that skill in thinking is developed as the by-product of attention to specific subject areas such as Geography and History is no longer tenable. Some thinking skills concerned with the sorting of information can be taught as a by-product of such subjects but these are only part of the broad range of thinking skills required in life. For example the thinking required for action must include consideration of priorities, objectives, other people's views and the like. **Descriptive thinking is not enough**.

It used to be felt that a person with a high IQ would necessarily be an effective thinker. This does not seem to be the case. Some people with high IQs turn out to be relatively ineffective thinkers and others with much more humble IQs are more effective. I have defined thinking as: **The operating skill with which intelligence acts upon experience**.

If IQ is the innate horsepower of a car then thinking skill is equivalent to driving skill. Because of this realization many schools for the exceptionally gifted are now using the **CoRT** Thinking Lessons in a deliberate attempt to avoid the "intelligence trap" which occurs when a high IQ is not accompanied by effective thinking skills.

To be effective, thinking does require an information base. But it is absurd to suppose that if we have enough information it will do our thinking for us. Only in very rare instances can we ever have such complete information that thinking is superfluous. In most cases we have to supplement inadequate information by use of our thinking skills. I have lectured to hundreds of thousands of industrialists, scientists, engineers, architects, teachers, public servants, and many other groups. Again and again there arises the complaint that nowhere in their education had they been taught how to think.

There need not be any complicated mystique about thinking. The **CoRT** Lessons have been designed to be practical and usable, in a wide variety of situations ranging from the jungles of Venezuela to IBM corporate headquarters in Paris. They have been used in elite schools and in schools in disadvantaged areas. On the whole they have been used by teachers who have not had any previous training in the use of the lessons. The basic format allows the lessons to be used over a wide range of ages (6 years to adult) and abilities (IQs of 75 to 140). This is not as surprising as it may seem, for the **CoRT** lessons are concerned with the basic thinking processes and these are the same at any age. The lessons are designed to be simple and practical.

In teaching the **CoRT** lessons the idiom is: **simple, practical, clear, focused and serious.** At all times the teacher must avoid over-complication and confusion. Both teacher and students must have a clear idea of what they are doing. The emphasis is on practicality not on exotic philosophizing. Examples and illustrations must be clear. The teacher must focus very sharply on the aspect of thinking that is being learned. This is the opposite of waffle, drift and "interesting" discussion. The idiom of training in a sport is not inappropriate. Above all the teacher must be serious about the importance of teaching thinking directly as a basic skill. It is not something to be dabbled in in an off-hand experimental way.

The general method used is what I call the "glasses method." If you have poor eyesight then you cannot see the world clearly. With glasses you see the world clearly and as a result your actions are more appropriate and your behavior more effective. The specific purpose of the **CoRT 1** lessons is to **broaden perception** so that in any thinking situation we can see beyond the obvious, immediate and egocentric. Experience has shown that students who have been through the lessons develop a much broader view of situations.

Edward de Bono

AUTHOR'S NOTE

Many years' experience with these materials has taught me that teachers will want to use these Teacher's Notes in two distinct ways. The first is as a guide to the specific lessons. The second is an an introduction to the subject of teaching thinking in general and also to the particular method used here. The teacher should if possible read the section "Teaching Method" (page 44) before starting the lessons. However, once this background material has been read it becomes of less importance than the actual guidelines for running the individual lessons. It is for this reason that "Teaching Method" follows the instructions for the lessons in this book.

As an additional aid to teaching the lessons, teachers are referred to the section "A Model Lesson Sequence" (page 7), which consists of a one-page outline of the lesson style.

A MODEL LESSON SEQUENCE

ONE

Do not mention the subject of the lesson, but start with a story or an exercise which illustrates the aspect of thinking that is the subject of the lesson.

TWO

Introduce the TOOL or SUBJECT of the lesson and explain simply what it does. You can use the introduction in the student workcards.

THREE

Carry out an open class example by setting a task and asking for individual responses. Repeat the letters of the tool or the subject as often as you can.

FOUR

Divide the class into groups of 4, 5 or 6. Set a practice item from the student workcards. Allow about three minutes or the time specified.

FIVE

Get feedback from the groups, for example by getting one suggestion from each of the groups (see also page 45).

SIX

Repeat the thinking with another item. Repeat practice items in this manner. Allow time to discuss the process of the lesson.

SEVEN

Use the principles given in the student workcards to have a discussion around the tool or subject of the lesson. If this discussion is weak, plug in a final practice item.

EIGHT

If it is customary to give homework, use one of the project items for this purpose.

For full details on the Standard Lesson Format, the teacher may wish to see *page 52*.

LESSON NOTES – HOW TO RUN THE LESSONS

On the following pages are sets of lesson notes to accompany the **CoRT** student workcards. In practice, teachers should read through the lesson notes before the lesson and mark the items they are going to use. During the lesson itself the teacher should use the lesson notes in conjunction with the student workcards which appear as insets alongside the lesson notes.

NOTES ON STARRING: ✭

The practice items throughout the **CoRT** Thinking Lessons have been carefully designed to be usable across a broad range of ages and abilities. Naturally, a higher degree of thinking skill is demanded from the more able student even if the practice item is the same. Some of the practice items are starred in order to show that these items are more suitable for older students. This does not mean that they cannot be used with younger students but that the teacher should use the other items first. In the same way, the unstarred items can also be used with older and more able students. As has been indicated elsewhere, teachers are encouraged to modify the items and to adapt them to local circumstances or news items.

HOW TO RUN
A **PMI** LESSON

PMI: Plus, Minus, Interesting

THE TREATMENT OF IDEAS

The **PMI** is a crystallization of the open-minded attitude into a tool that can be used deliberately. This is a very basic lesson which is introduced right at the beginning so that the **PMI** process itself can be used as a tool in the course of subsequent lessons. Instead of just deciding whether or not you like an idea, this thinking operation has you make an effort to find the good points (**P=Plus**), the bad points (**M=Minus**) and the interesting points (**I=Interesting**) about an idea. The interesting points are those which are neither good nor bad but are worth noticing. The **PMI** is a way of treating ideas, suggestions and proposals. The natural reaction to an idea is to like or dislike it, to approve or disapprove. If you like an idea, it is very unnatural to look for the negative or minus aspects. If you dislike an idea it is very unnatural to look for the positive or plus aspects. It is equally unnatural to pick out the merely interesting aspects of an idea.

Using the **PMI** as a deliberate operation gives students a means of by-passing the natural emotional reaction to an idea. Their objectives change from emotional reactions to carrying out with skill a formal operation.

Once the **PMI** has been practiced as a tool it can be asked for in subsequent lessons: "Do a **PMI** on that idea."

> The **PMI** is never intended to prevent decision or commitment but to ensure that this happens after both sides of the matter have been considered and **not** before.

In simple terms the **PMI** operation enlarges the view of a situation; without it, emotional reaction to an idea narrows the way we look at it.

See inset of the student workcard for an example of a **PMI** *on the idea that all seats should be taken out of buses.*

Further example: Windows should be made of transparent plastic instead of glass.

P: They would not break as easily.
They would not be as dangerous when broken.

M: Plastic would be more expensive than glass.
Plastic would get scratched very easily.

I: Perhaps windows could be of all colors if they were plastic.
Perhaps we take it for granted that glass is best since we are used to it.

PMI: THE TREATMENT OF IDEAS

P=Plus. The good things about an idea – why you like it

M=Minus. The bad things about an idea – why you don't like it

I=Interest. What you find interesting about an idea

Instead of just saying that you like an idea, or don't like it, you can use a **PMI**. When you use a **PMI** you give the good points first, then the bad points, and then the points which are neither good nor bad, but are interesting. You can use a **PMI** as a way of treating ideas, suggestions and proposals. You can ask someone else to do a **PMI** on an idea or you may be asked to do one yourself.

EXAMPLE

Idea: All the seats should be taken out of buses.

P: More people can get into each bus.
It would be easier to get in and out.
Buses would be cheaper to make and to repair.

M: Passengers would fall over if the bus stopped suddenly.
Old people and disabled people would not be able to use buses.
It would be difficult to carry shopping bags or babies.

I: Interesting idea that might lead to two types of bus, one with and one without seats.
Interesting idea that the same bus would do more work.
Interesting idea that comfort may not be so important in a bus.

PRACTICE

1. By law all cars should be painted bright yellow.

2. People should wear badges showing whether they are in a good mood or bad mood that day.

3. All students should spend 3 months every year earning money.

4. Every adult should spend one week a year in the police force.

5. There should be a special TV channel for young people only.

★ 6. In many countries there is a jury system in which ordinary people assess whether an accused person is guilty or not. Some other countries do not have juries but have three judges who do all the assessment themselves. Do a **PMI** on this three-judge system.

★ 7. Do a **PMI** on the system which allows a lawyer to sue on behalf of a client and then to take a percentage of the damages awarded by the courts. If the lawyer does win the case, then he charges no fee.

PROCESS

DISCUSSION

- When is a **PMI** most useful?
- Does one always look at the good and bad points of an idea?
- Does a **PMI** waste time?
- Is it easy to do a **PMI**?

PRINCIPLES

A. The **PMI** is important because without it you may reject a valuable idea that seems bad at first sight.

B. Without a **PMI** you are very unlikely to see the disadvantages of an idea that you like very much.

C. The **PMI** can show that ideas are not just good or bad but can also be interesting if they lead to other ideas.

D. Without a **PMI** most judgments are based not on the value of the idea itself but on your emotions at that time.

E. With a **PMI** you decide whether or not you like the idea after you have explored it instead of before.

PROJECT

1. All cars should be banned from city centers so that people can walk about freely.

2. Every young person should adopt an old person to care for.

★ 3. People should be allowed to work 10 hours a day for 4 days and have the rest of the week free, instead of working 8 hours a day for 5 days.

ISBN 0 08-034446-1

PRACTICE

*(see **Practice** section in inset of student workcard)*

Normally practice items 1, 2 and 3 are used one after the other. But a teacher may choose to substitute items 4–7 for any of these. The students work in groups as usual.

PRACTICE ITEM 1. Here each group does a full **PMI** for 3–5 minutes. One group is then designated to give its **Plus** points and the other groups or individuals can add further points. Another group is then designated to give its **Minus** points and finally a further group is designated to give its **Interesting** points.

Suggestions:

P: Yellow cars would be easier to see at night or in fog, so there would be fewer accidents.
Car showrooms would be able to let you have the car immediately instead of your having to wait for the color you want.
Cars would be more likely to be treated as a means of transport than as status symbols.

M: It would be rather boring.
Paint manufacturers and advertisers would have a hard time.
It would be difficult for the police to chase a particular car or trace stolen ones.

I: Should the car color be of use to the owner or to everyone else?
Do people drive different colored cars differently?

PRACTICE ITEM 2. Here each group again does a full **PMI** but this time the objective is to try to guess the two **Plus** points, the two **Minus** points, and the two **Interesting** points which the teacher holds. Time allowed is 3–5 minutes, at the end of which each group can offer one suggestion at a time for either **P, M,** or **I** points, when a group guesses one of the target points given below, the teacher indicates this. When no more points are forthcoming the teacher gives out the remaining target points.

Target Points:

P: You could steer clear of people in a bad mood.
People might make more of an effort not to be in a bad mood if it was going to show.

M: People would not be honest about wearing the right badge.
People in a bad mood who needed cheering up would be avoided instead.

I: With some people you can tell their mood from their faces anyway.
Do people prefer to hide their moods or to show them?

PRACTICE ITEM 3. Here individual groups do either **P** points, **M** points or **I** points as instructed by the teacher. Time allowed is 3 minutes. One group is then designated to give the **P** points, another to give the **M** points and another to give the **I** points. In each case the other groups can add further points as they wish.

PROCESS

*(see **Process** section in inset of student workcard)*

Open discussion with the class as a whole, acting as individuals rather than groups.
● When is a **PMI** most useful?
● Does one always look at the good and bad points of an idea?
● Does a **PMI** waste time?
● Is it easy to do a **PMI**?
This discussion should last about five minutes before the class moves on to the next section.

PRINCIPLES

*(see **Principles** section in inset of student workcard)*

The groups look at the list of principles given in the student notes. They are asked to pick out the principle they think is the most important. The groups can also be asked to criticize any one of the principles or to make up a principle of their own.

PROJECT

*(see **Project** section in inset of student workcard)*

In single-period lessons there will not be time for this section. The project items can be used as essay topics or given to students to work on in their own time in schools where this is customary. In longer lessons the groups can work on a project item chosen by them or the teacher, as described in the standard lesson format section.

HOW TO RUN A **CAF** LESSON

CAF: Consider All Factors

THE FACTORS INVOLVED

CAF is a crystallization of the process of trying to consider all the factors in a situation.

> This thinking operation is essentially related to action, decision, planning, judgment, and coming to a conclusion.

People naturally assume that they have considered all the factors, but usually their consideration is limited to the obvious ones. Turning **CAF** into a deliberate operation switches attention from the importance of the factors to looking around for **all the factors**. Clearly it is difficult to consider all the factors, so in the teaching situation consideration can be limited to the ten most important factors (or any other number), or the lesson can be taught in terms of:

- the factors affecting oneself
- the factors affecting other people
- the factors affecting society in general.

This gives the lesson structure.

The emphasis of the lesson is on the factors that have been left out in a decision, plan, etc. In doing a **CAF**, students try to ensure that all important factors are listed. In looking at each other's thinking, students try to spot which factors have been neglected. The **CAF** may be applied to one's own thinking as well as to the thinking of others: "What factors have I left out here?"

CAF differs from **PMI** in that **PMI** is a reaction to an idea whereas **CAF** is an exploration of a situation before coming up with an idea. The two do sometimes overlap because some of the factors that have to be considered obviously have a plus or minus aspect. The intention with a **CAF** is to be **as complete as possible** and to consider all factors rather than looking at them in terms of favorable or unfavorable factors.

See student workcard for an example of what happened when a big city's traffic planners failed to do a **CAF** and left out a very important factor.

(NOTE: Logically it could be argued that **CAF** should come before **PMI**, since **CAF** includes **PMI** as it includes **C&S, OPV**, etc. But the **PMI** is the easier lesson to teach, so it comes first.)

The **CAF** lesson is a difficult one to teach because it is difficult to try and consider all factors. **The emphasis must therefore be on what has been left out**. For instance, each group tries to find factors that have not been put forward by the "designated group."

CAF: THE FACTORS INVOLVED

CAF=Consider All Factors.

When you have to choose or make a decision or just think about something, there are always many factors that you have to consider. If you leave out some of these factors, your choice may seem right at the time but will later turn out to be wrong. When you are looking at other people's thinking, you can try and see what factors they have left out.

EXAMPLE

Some years ago in a big city there was a law that all new buildings had to have large parking lots in the basement so that the people working in the building would have somewhere to park. After a while this law was changed because it was found to be a bad mistake. Why?

They had forgotten to consider the factor that providing parking lots would encourage everyone to drive in to work in their cars and so the traffic congestion on the road was worse than ever.

PRACTICE

1. A husband and wife go to buy a used car for their family. They consider all the following factors:

   That the person selling it actually owns it.
   The price of the car.
   The type of car and the color.
   The engine power and the speed of the car.
   That all the mechanical parts are working perfectly.
   That it is big enough for the family.

PRACTICE (continued)

2. Do a full **CAF** on the factors involved in choosing a career.

3. An inventor has invented a breakfast pill which is very tiny but contains all the food and vitamins you need. After you have eaten the pill you do not feel hungry for five hours. Should this pill be allowed. What are the factors involved?

4. What are the factors involved in choosing your hairstyle?

5. If you were interviewing someone to be a teacher, what factors would you consider?

⭐ 6. The textile workers in a country demand protection from foreign imports which are coming into the country at a lower price and taking over the market. What factors should a government consider in this matter?

⭐ 7. There is a plan to turn a golf course on the edge of a growing town into a new shopping center. This is backed by business and the consumers but opposed by environmentalists. What factors should be considered in the final decision?

PROCESS

Discussion:

- Is it easy to leave out important factors?
- When is it most important to consider all the factors?
- What is the difference between **PMI** and **CAF**?
- What happens when other people leave out certain factors?
- Do you need to consider all factors or only the most important ones?

PRINCIPLES

A. Doing a **CAF** is useful before choosing, deciding or planning.

B. It is better to consider all the factors first and then pick out the ones that matter most.

C. You may have to ask someone else to tell you whether you have left out some important factors.

D. If you have left out an important factor your answer may seem right but will later turn out to be wrong.

E. If you do a **CAF** on someone else's thinking you may be able to tell the person what has been left out.

PROJECT

1. What factors should you consider in designing a chair?

⭐ 2. A young couple is undecided whether to get married at once or wait. What factors should they be considering?

3. In deciding how to spend your vacations, what factors would you consider?

ISBN 0 08-034446-1

PRACTICE

*(see **Practice** section in inset of student workcard)*

Normally practice items 1, 2 and 3 are used one after the other. But for any one of these the teacher may choose to substitute items 4 or 5. The students should work in groups.

PRACTICE ITEM 1. The groups spend 3 minutes trying to find factors which the couple buying the car has left out. The teacher then asks one group to give its findings and the other groups can then add other factors.

Suggestions:

- Their children may not like the car.
- Although they can afford to buy the car they may not be able to afford to run it if the gas consumption is very high.
- The car may not fit their garage (if they have one).

PRACTICE ITEM 2. Here the groups consider all the factors involved in choosing a career. They should spend 5–7 minutes on this. At the end of this time the teacher designates one group to give its output and then the other groups and individuals can add further points. If possible and if there is time, the points can all be listed on the blackboard and each group can pick out the four points it considers to be the most important.

PRACTICE ITEM 3. This is a quick item. The teacher gives the starting signal and in the next two minutes each group must pick out as many factors as it can. The groups who say they have picked out the highest number then give their output to which the others can add. This is a race to pick out the most factors in the shortest time.

Suggestions:

- Can one be sure that the breakfast pill contains all the food ingredients, even the ones we do not know about?
- What would happen to all the farmers, food manufacturers and shops?
- There would be no dishes to wash.
- You could have your breakfast while going to work.
- Breakfast would not be very enjoyable and people need enjoyment.
- Would people's stomachs shrink?
- If the pill were useful for breakfast wouldn't it be useful for every meal? Would this be safe?

PROCESS

*(see **Process** section in inset of student workcard)*

Open discussion with the class as a whole, acting as individuals rather than groups.

- Is it easy to leave out important factors?
- When is it most important to consider all the factors?
- What is the difference between **PMI** and **CAF**?
- What happens when other people leave out certain factors?
- Do you need to consider all factors or only the most important ones?

PRINCIPLES

*(see **Principles** section in inset of student workcard)*

The groups look at the list of principles given in the student's workcard. They are asked to pick out the principles they think most important. The groups can also be asked to criticize any one of the principles or to make up a principle of their own.

PROJECT
*(see **Project** section in inset of student workcard)*

When only a single period is allowed for the lesson there will not be time for this section. The project items can be used as essay subjects or given to the students for them to work on in their own time. In longer lessons the group can work on a project item chosen by them or the teacher as described in the standard lesson format section.

HOW TO RUN A **RULES** LESSON

RULES

The main purpose of this lesson is to provide an opportunity for practicing the two previous lessons: **PMI** and **CAF**. **Rules** provide a neat and well-defined thinking situation. An existing or proposed rule is an opportunity for practicing **PMI**. The factors involved in making a rule provide an opportunity for practicing **CAF**.

Although the main purpose of the lesson is to provide this practice opportunity, some attention must also be paid to rules in their own right as part of the thinking situation. In thinking about anything, there are usually various rules that have to be followed or cannot be broken among the factors to be considered. Another reason for introducing rules here is to counteract the notion that there are no rules in the thinking lessons and that anything goes.

The intention is **not** to have a philosophical discussion about rules but to use **Rules** as something to think about. As long as the emphasis of the lesson is on thinking about rules, some discussion can be centered on **Rules** themselves, especially in the process discussion section.

(see student workcard inset for a brief explanation of rules)

PRACTICE

*(see **Practice** section in inset of student workcard)*

Normally practice items 1, 2 and 3 and are used one after the other. A teacher may, however, choose to use practice items 4–7 instead of any one of these. The students work in groups, as usual.

PRACTICE ITEM 1. The groups spend 5 minutes trying to produce four rules for parents. At the end of this period each group in turn is asked for one rule until no further ones are forthcoming.

Suggestions:

- Parents should listen more.
- Parents should try to see things from a young person's point of view.
- Parents should not quarrel in front of their children.
- Parents should let children make some decisions for themselves.
- Parents should tell children from time to time what they do not like about them.

RULES

- Some rules are made to prevent confusion: for example, the rule that cars must drive on one side of the road.
- Some rules are made to be enjoyed: for example, the rules of football make the game of football.
- Some rules are made by organizations for their own members: for example, the rule that soldiers must wear uniforms when on duty.
- Some rules are made to prevent a few people from taking advantage of everyone else: for example, the rule that you must not steal.
- In general, the purpose of a rule is to make life easier and better for the majority of people.

PRACTICE

1. You are a member of a committee which is trying to set up some rules for parents to obey when dealing with their children. Can you think of four main rules?

2. Do a **PMI** on the rules produced for parents in the preceding problem.

★3. In most countries, cars are driven on the right-hand side of the road. In Britain, however, they are driven on the left-hand side. There is a suggestion that Britain should change from the left-hand side to the right-hand side to be like other countries. What are the factors involved? Do a **CAF** on this situation.

4. A group of people sails away to an island to start a new life. They abolish money, property and all the old rules. They soon find that no one wants to do the hard work needed to grow food and build houses. Do a **CAF** on this situation and then invent some rules.

PRACTICE (*continued*)

5. A new rule is suggested for marriages. Instead of being married for ever, the participants can be married for five or ten years as they wish. Do a **PMI** on this idea.

★6. There is concern that young people may buy and watch video tapes that are too full of violence and are not suitable for them. What rules could you devise to protect against this happening?

7. In a sailing boat race there are all sorts of boats. Some are big and fast. Some are small and slower. You want everyone to have a chance of winning. What rules could you set up?

PROCESS

Discussion:

- Which rules are good and which are bad?
- Who makes rules?
- What are rules for?
- When are rules useful?

PRINCIPLES

A. A rule should be widely known and understood and also possible to obey.

B. A rule is not a bad rule just because some people do not like it.

continued

PRINCIPLES (*continued*)

C. A rule should work for the benefit of most of those who have to obey it.

D. Those who have to obey a rule should be able to see its purpose.

E. From time to time rules should be examined to see if they still make sense.

PROJECT

1. If you were running a school, which rules would you insist on?

2. If you were organizing a competition for finding the champion sausage eater, what rules would you make for this competition?

★3. Should there be any rules for industrial strikes?

ISBN 0 08-034446-1

© 1986 Mica Management Resources (UK) Inc. All Rights Reserved. No part of this publication may be reproduced, stored in a retrieval system or transmitted in any form or by any means: electronic, electrostatic, magnetic tape, mechanical, photocopying, recording or otherwise, without permission in writing from the publishers.

CoRT 1
WORKCARD 3

CoRT THINKING

BREADTH

RULES

EDWARD DE BONO

PERGAMON PRESS
NEW YORK · OXFORD · BEIJING · FRANKFURT · SÃO PAULO · SYDNEY · TOKYO · TORONTO

PRACTICE ITEM 2. A single rule is picked out from the preceding result and fed back to the groups to do a **PMI** on. Time allowed is 3 minutes. At the end of this time one group is designated to give its output and the other groups can add further points.

PRACTICE ITEM 3. With this practice item emphasize the difference between **PMI** and **CAF**. The groups are asked to make a **CAF** list of the factors involved – not to indicate whether or not it is a good idea. Time allowed is 3 minutes. The group with the longest **CAF** list gives its output, to which the others can add. The list can be written on a blackboard or an overhead-projector can be used.

Suggestions:

- Changing traffic signs around.
- Re-educating people.
- Accidents because people would forget on which side to drive.
- Perhaps increased sales of foreign cars.
- Bus stops would have to be moved.

PROCESS

*(see **Process** section in inset of student workcard)*

Open discussion with the class as a whole, acting as individuals rather than groups.

- Which rules are good and which are bad?
- Who makes rules?
- What are rules for?
- When are rules useful?

PRINCIPLES

*(see **Principles** section in inset of student workcard)*

The groups look at the list of principles given in the student workcards. They are asked to pick out the principle they think is most important. The groups can also be asked to criticize any one of the principles or make up a principle of their own.

PROJECT

*(see **Project** section in inset of student workcard)*

When only a single period is allowed for the lessons there will not be time for this section. The project items can be used as essay subjects or given to the students for them to work on in their own time. In longer lessons the groups can work on a project item chosen by them or by the teacher as described in the standard lesson format section.

HOW TO RUN A **C&S** LESSON

C&S: Consequence and Sequel

FOCUS ON THE CONSEQUENCES

> **C&S** is a crystallization of the process of looking ahead to see the consequences of some action, plan, decision, rule, invention etc.

For some people, thinking ahead may always be part of doing a **CAF**, but it is worth emphasizing this process more directly since **consequences do not exist until you make an effort to foresee them, whereas factors are always present at the moment. CAF** is primarily concerned with factors that are operating at the moment and on which a decision is based, whereas **C&S** deals with what may happen after the decision has been made. There are immediate consequences as well as short-term (1–5 years), medium-term (5–25 years) and long-term consequences (over 25 years).

C&S is concerned with action of some sort, either the action that one intends to take oneself or the action that others are taking. The intention is to enlarge the view beyond the immediate effect of that action. An action may seem worthwhile if the immediate effect is good. But if one makes a deliberate effort to look at longer term consequences, the action may not be worthwhile at all. Conversely, an action that has good long-term consequences may not seem very enticing at the moment.

If **CAF** is thinking about a situation at the moment, then **C&S** is thinking ahead. Obviously, consequences also can turn up as part of a **PMI**, but **the important point about a deliberate C&S is that attention is focused directly on the future.**

PRACTICE ITEM 1. Each group is asked to do a different time scale **C&S**. One group does immediate consequences, another short-term, another medium-term and another long-term consequences. Where there are more than four groups the process is repeated. Time allowed is 3 minutes. One group for each time scale is designated to give its output and the others can add further points as usual.

Suggestions:

- Immediate consequences include massive unemployment and misery, opposition to the idea, strikes, etc.
- Short-term consequences include shift into service industries, re-training and changes in the method of distributing income.
- Medium-term consequences might include the idea of two people for every job (taking turns), hobbies, crafts and boredom.
- Long-term consequences might include people only working for two months a year – rather like a reverse vacation.

20

C&S: CONSEQUENCES

C&S = Consequence and Sequel

The invention of the gasoline engine made possible automobiles, airplanes, the oil industry and a great deal of pollution. If all the consequences could have been forseen at the time, electric or steam engines might have been used in cars. A new invention, a plan, a rule or a decision all have consequences that go on for a long time. In thinking about an action, the consequences should always be considered:

Immediate consequences

Short-term consequences   (1-5 years)

Medium-term consequences   (5-25 years)

Long-term consequences   (over 25 years)

EXAMPLE

A man introduced rabbits to Australia to provide hunting for his friends. The immediate consequences were good because his friends had plenty to shoot at. The short-term consequences were also good because the rabbit provided an alternative source of meat. The medium-term consequences were bad because the rabbit multiplied so much that it became a pest. The long-term consequences were very bad because the rabbit spread all over Australia and did a great deal of damage to crops.

PRACTICE

1. A new electronic robot is invented to replace all human labor in factories. The invention is announced. Do a **C&S** on this.

PRACTICE (continued)

2. A new law is suggested to allow school children to leave school and start earning a living as soon as they want to after the age of 12. Do a **C&S** on this from the point of view of someone who leaves early, from the point of view of the schools, and from the point of view of society in general.

3. A new device makes it possible to tell whenever someone is telling a lie. Do an immediate **C&S** on this.

⭐ 4. While a boy is away on vacation his best friend goes off with his girl friend. What do you think would happen when the boy got back?

⭐ 5. There is a quiet residential district. Offices start opening in the area. Then there are more and more offices. What will change? Do an immediate and short-term **C&S** on this.

6. Some new medical evidence suggests that people who are slightly overweight are more healthy than people who are underweight. What consequences do you think this would have?

⭐ 7. The price of houses and even of condominiums rises to the point where young people cannot afford to buy them. What do you think will happen? Do a full **C&S**.

PROCESS

Discussion:

● Do long-term consequences matter?

● If it is not easy to see the consequences, should you bother with them?

● When is it most useful to look at them?

● Whose business is it to look at consequences?

PRINCIPLES

A. Other people may be able to see the consequences of your action more easily than you can yourself.

B. It is important to know whether the consequences are reversible or not.

C. The immediate consequences and the long-term consequences may be opposite: immediate consequences may be good and long-term consequences bad, or the other way round.

D. You should look at the consequences not only as they affect you but as they affect other people as well.

E. You should do a full **C&S** before deciding which consequences you should consider.

PROJECT

⭐ 1. The world runs out of oil and gas. What would happen?

2. All school examinations are abolished. Do a **C&S** on this.

3. What are the consequences of arguing with your parents?

ISBN 0 08-034446-1

© 1986 Mica Management Resources (UK) Inc. All Rights Reserved. No part of this publication may be reproduced, stored in a retrieval system or transmitted in any form or by any means: electronic, electrostatic, magnetic tape, mechanical, photocopying, recording or otherwise, without permission in writing from the publishers.

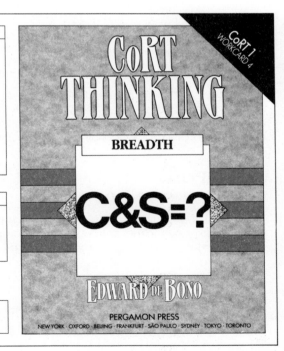

CoRT 1
WORKCARD 4

CoRT THINKING

BREADTH

C&S=?

EDWARD DE BONO

PERGAMON PRESS

NEW YORK · OXFORD · BEIJING · FRANKFURT · SÃO PAULO · SYDNEY · TOKYO · TORONTO

PRACTICE ITEM 2. Each group chooses which point of view it is going to explore with a **C&S:** the point of view of someone who leaves school early, the schools themselves or society in general. At the end of 3 minutes an output is invited from each of the points of view by means of designated groups. If one point of view has not been chosen it can be briefly discussed.

Suggestions:

- The children who do not like school will leave early and may soon make a lot of money.
- If they are successful they will not regret it but if unsuccessful they might.
- There might be pressure from parents to make children leave school early.
- The schools might benefit since those remaining would really want to be in school rather than being there because they are forced to.
- Society would probably suffer because there would be wide differences in education among its members.
- Those who left early might not find it easy to move to a different job if the one they were doing became obsolete.

PRACTICE ITEM 3. Only 1 minute is allowed for the groups to consider this practice item. At the end of that time the teacher moves from group to group getting one suggestion at a time until no new ideas are forthcoming.

Suggestions:

- Courts and legal procedures would be greatly simplified.
- Police could round up a lot of suspects and question each one.
- People would quickly learn to tell half-truths.
- Perhaps it would not make much difference because the machine would only be used if you suspected the person was lying.
- On the whole, people would be better behaved.

PROCESS
*(see **Process** section in inset of student workcard)*

Open discussion with the class as a whole, acting as individuals rather than groups.

- Do long–term consequences matter?
- If it is not easy to see the consequences should you bother with them?
- When is it most useful to look at the consequences?
- Whose business is it to look at consequences?

PRINCIPLES
*(see **Principles** section in inset of student workcard)*

The groups look at the list of principles given in the student workcards. They are asked to pick out the principle they think is most important. The groups can also be asked to criticize any one of the principles or to make up a principle of their own.

PROJECT
*(see **Project** section in inset of student workcard)*

When only a single period is allowed for the lessons there will not be time for this section. The project items can be used as essay topics or for students to work on in their own time. In longer lessons the groups can work on a project item chosen by themselves or by the teacher as described in the standard lesson format section.

HOW TO RUN
AN **AGO** LESSON

AGO: Aims, Goals, Objectives

FOCUS ON PURPOSE

In some situations, it is more appropriate to speak of aims, in other circumstances of goals, and in yet others of objectives. **The main point of the lesson is to introduce and emphasize the idea of purpose**. No attempt should be made to bring out the philosophical differences between these since this usually confuses students.

This notion of purpose broadens the perception of a situation. The **AGO** is a device to get students to focus directly and deliberately on **the intention behind actions**. What is the actor aiming for? What is trying to be achieved? What does the actor want to bring about? What are the actor's objectives? What are the actor's goals?

> Being able to define objectives helps the student's thinking in such areas as decision, planning, and action of any kind which has a purpose.

It is enough for the teacher to say that in some cases the word **aim** is more appropriate and in other cases **goals** or **objectives**. If pressed, teachers can make the distinction as follows:

- aim is the general direction
- goal is an ultimate destination
- objective is a recognizable point of achievement along the way.

Teachers are strongly advised to concentrate on the general idea of "purpose" and not to make the distinction. Without a sense of purpose, all actions are either reactions to a situation or matters of habit or imitation. **The intention of the lesson is to focus attention directly on purpose as distinct from reaction.**

PRACTICE
*(see **Practice** section in inset of student workcard)*

Normally practice items 1, 2, and 3 are used one after the other. But a teacher may substitute practice items 4–7 as wished. The students work in groups.

PRACTICE ITEM 1. Only 2 minutes are allowed for this practice item and then the teacher asks the groups in turn to give a possible explanation. When a number of explanations have been given the teacher should distinguish between the "because" explanations and the "in order" explanations.

AGO: OBJECTIVES

AGO = Aims, Goals, Objectives

You can do something out of habit, because everyone else is doing it, or as a reaction to a situation. These are all "because" reasons. But there are also times when you do something "in order to" achieve some purpose or objective. It can help your thinking if you know exactly what you are trying to achieve. It can also help you to understand other people's thinking if you can see their objectives. In certain situations the words "aims" and "goals" are more appropriate than objectives, but the meaning is the same.

EXAMPLE

A developer who is building a large new shopping center has the objective of making a profit for his corporation and for himself as a result. He also has the objective of putting up a shopping center that will be successful. He must have the objective of pleasing the potential shoppers. He must have the objective of fitting in with the planning authorities. In addition, he has the objective of working so well (on time and within budget) that he will be asked to develop more shopping centers in other places.

PRACTICE

1. A father is very angry with his daughter, so he doubles her allowance. Why do you think he did this?

2. What would your objectives be if you won $5,000.00 on a game show?

PRACTICE (continued)

★ 3. Everyone has to eat to live. But people have different objectives with regard to food. Do an **AGO** for the following people: homemaker, cook, store owner, food manufacturer, farmer, government.

4. Do an **AGO** for the police and put the objectives in order of priority.

5. You are the commander of a spacecraft approaching Earth from another planet. What different objectives might you have? Do three alternative **AGO**s.

★ 6. You are a dealer selling Ford motor cars. Another Ford dealer in a nearby town lowers his prices so that they are below yours. What are you going to do about it? What are your objectives?

7. What are your objectives when you turn on the TV?

PROCESS

Discussion:
- Is it always necessary to know your objectives exactly?
- When is it most useful to know the objectives?
- What happens if you do not have objectives?
- How important are other people's objectives?

PRINCIPLES

A. If you know exactly what your objectives are, it is easier to achieve them.

B. In the same situation different people may have different objectives.

C. On the way to a final objective, there may be a chain of smaller objectives, each one following from the previous one.

D. Objectives should be near enough, real enough and possible enough for a person to really try to reach them.

E. There may be many objectives, but some are more important than others.

PROJECT

★ 1. What is the difference between the **AGO** of a politician and the **AGO** of a business executive? Examine the points of difference and the points of similarity.

2. You are setting out to design a completely new type of house. What would your objectives be?

3. What are the objectives of a school principal?

ISBN 0 08-034446-1

© 1986 Mica Management Resources (UK) Inc. All Rights Reserved. No part of this publication may be reproduced, stored in a retrieval system or transmitted in any form or by any means: electronic, electrostatic, magnetic tape, mechanical, photocopying, recording or otherwise, without permission in writing from the publishers.

CoRT 1 WORKCARD 5

CoRT THINKING

BREADTH

AGO

EDWARD DE BONO

PERGAMON PRESS
NEW YORK · OXFORD · BEIJING · FRANKFURT · SÃO PAULO · SYDNEY · TOKYO · TORONTO

Suggestions:

- Because the girl had been stealing money.
- Because he was sorry he had been angry with her.
- In order to show her that he could still love her and be angry at the same time.
- In order to have her go to the movies more often and avoid any domestic tension.
- In order to give him something to take away when he was angry again.

PRACTICE ITEM 2. Time allowed is 3 minutes. One group is designated to give its output and then the other groups can add points or comments. The emphasis here should be on trying to condense the different objectives into major categories; for instance: having fun, helping others, saving, investing, buying equipment to make money as with tools, paying for education.

PRACTICE ITEM 3. Each group is given one of the types to do an **AGO** for. If there are more than six groups the process is repeated and if there are fewer some types are left out. At the end of 3 minutes one group for each type gives its output and the others can comment or add to it.

Suggestions:

- Homemaker – to buy enough food within its budget.
- Cook – to find the right quality food and variety.
- Shopkeepers – to satisfy their customers and to make enough money to live on.
- Manufacturer – to sell as much as possible and make as much profit as possible.
- Farmers – to get a proper return for their work and a stable market.
- Government – to ensure food supplies and keep prices down.

PROCESS
*(see **Process** section in inset of student workcard)*

Open discussion with the class as a whole, acting as individuals rather than in groups.

- Is it necessary to know your objectives exactly, always?
- When is it most useful to know the objectives?
- What happens if you do not have objectives?
- How important are other people's objectives?

PRINCIPLES
*(see **Principles** section in inset of student workcard)*

The groups look at the list of principles given in the student workcards. They are asked to pick out the principle they think is most important. The groups can also be asked to criticize any one of the principles or to make up a principle of their own.

PROJECT
*(see **Project** section in inset of student workcard)*

When only a single period is allowed for the lesson there will not be time for this section. The project items can be used as essay topics or given to the students to work on in their own time. In longer lessons the group can work on a project item chosen by them or the teacher as described in the standard lesson format section.

HOW TO RUN
A **PLANNING** LESSON

PLANNING

> The idea is to use planning as a thinking situation which brings together objectives (**AGO**), consequences (**C&S**), the factors involved (**CAF**), and the treatment of ideas (**PMI**).

It is not suggested that these are the only things involved in planning, but they are certainly among the more important things. Planning is also there in its own right as a definite thinking situation which requires some practice.

As in the **Rules** lesson, the emphasis is not so much on how to make plans but on the thinking operation that may be involved. No formula for making plans is put forward, but since consequences, objectives and factors all play so important a part in planning, attention to these aspects improves the ability to plan.

Although the lesson is not intended to be a general discussion of planning as such, enough attention should be paid to the process (especially in conducting the **discussion** and **principles** sections) for the student to develop some awareness of what planning involves and why it matters.

(See inset of student workcard for examples of planning. These can be elaborated if so desired.)

PRACTICE
*(see **Practice** section in inset of student workcard)*

Normally practice items 1, 2 and 3 would be used one after the other. Practice items 4–7 are given as alternatives should the teacher prefer to use them. Project items could also be used as alternatives. In this lesson the first three items are about the same problem.

PRACTICE ITEM 1. Half the groups do a **CAF** on the situation and the other half do an **AGO**. Time allowed is 3 minutes. At the end of this time one group is designated to give the **CAF** output and another group to give an **AGO** output. The other groups can add to these as usual. The points may be listed on a board.

PLANNING

Planning is thinking ahead to see how you are going to do something. It may be a matter of getting to some place or getting something done. It may be a matter of organizing things so that they run smoothly. In a plan you set up a program of what you are going to do. The more complicated the thing you are going to do, the more necessary it is to have a clear plan.

EXAMPLES

A general plans how he is going to win the battle.
A boy plans his holiday.
A football coach plans how he is going to win a match.
A family plans a picnic.
A railway manager plans how to organize the train schedule.
A girl plans her career when she leaves school.

PRACTICE

1. The center of a town has become a slum and the town council wants to do something about it. What are the factors involved and what objectives should they have? Do a **CAF** and an **AGO** for them.

⭐2. In the above problem what plan should they make? Put the plan into three stages.

⭐3. Do a short-term and a medium-term **C&S** on the plan given above.

PRACTICE (continued)

4. Your objective is to make money and you have the choice of any three of the things listed here: 5 bicycles, a horse, 2,000 old books, one ton of red paint, a printing machine, and a recipe for sausages. Make a plan showing how you would use your choice of three things.

⭐5. Devise a plan which would make it easier for people to find the jobs they like.

6. You agree to sell candles to raise money for charity and to make some money for yourself. How would you plan to do this? What factors would you have to consider?

7. A thief has been stealing things at a swimming pool. How would you plan to catch this thief?

PROCESS

Discussion:
- What is difficult about planning?
- When are plans necessary?
- What is the most important thing about planning?
- What are the disadvantages of having a plan?

PRINCIPLES

A. In planning it is important to know exactly what you want to achieve (**AGO**).

continued

PRINCIPLES (continued)

B. Always have an alternative plan ready in case something goes wrong with the first plan.

C. The value of a plan depends upon its consequences (**C&S**).

D. Keep the plan as simple and direct as possible.

E. Consider all factors (**CAF**) very carefully and get as much information as possible before making your plan.

PROJECT

1. You get permission to turn the school into a discotheque in the evenings. Make a plan showing how you would do it, and also do a **PMI** on the idea.

2. Large footprints in the snow in the Himalayas are supposed to be due to a mysterious creature called a Yeti. Plan an expedition to find out more about the Yeti and photograph it if possible.

⭐3. How would you prevent people from hijacking aircraft? Can you devise a plan to do this?

ISBN 0 08-034446-1

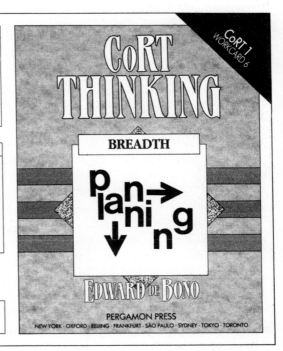

PERGAMON PRESS
NEW YORK · OXFORD · BEIJING · FRANKFURT · SÃO PAULO · SYDNEY · TOKYO · TORONTO

Suggestions:

CAF: Can the buildings be improved or are they beyond repair?
What is going to happen to the people living in the area?
What is going to happen to the cost of the work – who is going to pay for this?
Disruption of the rest of the town.
Should business be allowed into part of the area?
The amount of land available and the number of people involved.
Could people afford to pay rents in new houses, shops, etc?

AGO: To improve the well-being of the people living in the area.
To improve the town for everyone.
To stay within the available budget or raise funds.
To get everyone's cooperation, etc.

PRACTICE ITEM 2. All groups try to devise a plan to deal with the situation. To give some structure to the plan so that it is more than just a statement of intention a three-stage form is suggested (phases or steps). Time allowed is 3 minutes. Each group in turn then gives its plan very briefly.

Suggestions:

Stage I: find out what the people want, find out whether improvement or re-building is necessary, consider the costs and alternative plans.
Stage II: create new buildings in open spaces, and in a cautious manner replace buildings without having to move people out.
Stage III: when everyone is re-housed clean up the area to make it more attractive for the people to live there.

PRACTICE ITEM 3. Take one of the suggested plans or create a synthetic one from among the others. Reduce this to some definite proposal and then the groups do a short- and medium-term **C&S** (from 1–25 years). Time allowed is 3 minutes. At the end of this time a group is designated to give the output.

PROCESS
*(see **Process** section in inset of student workcard)*

Open discussion with the class as a whole, acting as individuals rather than groups.

- What is difficult about planning?
- When are plans necessary?
- What is the most important thing about planning?
- What are the disadvantages of having a plan?

PRINCIPLES
*(see **Principles** section in inset of student workcard)*

The groups look at the list of principles given in the student workcards. They are asked to pick out the principle they think is most important. The groups can also be asked to criticize any one of the principles or to make up a principle of their own.

PROJECT
*(see **Project** section in inset of student workcard)*

When only a single period is allowed for the lesson there will not be time for this section. The project items can be used as essay topics or given to the students to work on in their own time. In longer lessons the groups can work on a project item chosen by the teacher or by themselves as described in the standard lesson format section.

HOW TO RUN
A **FIP** LESSON

FIP: First Important Priorities

FOCUS ON PRIORITIES

In most of the other lessons, the effort has been directed towards generating as many ideas as possible: as wide a **PMI** as possible; as many factors as possible for a **CAF**; as comprehensive a **C&S** as possible; all the different objectives, etc. **FIP** is a crystallization of the process of picking out the most important ideas, factors, objectives, consequences, etc. Obviously some of these ideas are more important than others. The purpose of **FIP** is to restore the balance in a deliberate manner.

If you try to pick out only the most important points from the start, you will be able to see only a small part of the picture. But if you start by trying to see as large a picture as possible, then your eventual assessment of importance will be much more valid. This is why the **FIP** lesson comes late in the series.

Like the **PMI**, the **FIP** operation can be used in subsequent lessons or in other subject areas whenever some assessment of importance is required. If students turn up with ideas which are valid as ideas but not of great importance, they can be asked to do a **FIP** on the situation.

FIP is a judgment situation and there are no absolute answers. What one person believes to be most important another person may place far down the list of priorities. The intention of the lesson is to focus attention directly onto this assessment of importance. Once you can do a **FIP**, then you are free to generate as many ideas as you like. If you cannot do a **FIP**, then you are only able to consider ideas that have an obvious importance at first sight – and you may well never get to consider any other ideas at all.

(See inset of student workcard for an example of the priorities involved in lending someone some money.)

PRACTICE
*(see **Practice** items in inset of student workcard)*

Normally items 1, 2 and 3 are used one after the other. But for any one of these the teacher may choose to substitute items 4–7. Items from the project section may also be used as alternatives. The students work in groups.

PRACTICE ITEM 1. From the list of six factors each group picks out the top three priorities. These need not be given in the order of importance. The outputs can be given verbally by each group in turn. They can also be written down on a piece of paper so that the teacher can compare them and perhaps draw up a "voting" list on board. Time allowed is 3 minutes.

FIP: PRIORITIES

FIP = First Important Priorities

Some things are more important than others. Some factors are more important than others. Some objectives are more important than others. Some consequences are more important than others. In thinking about a situation, after you have generated a number of ideas, you have to decide which ones are the more important ones so that you can do something about them. After doing a **PMI**, **CAF**, **AGO** or **C&S**, you can do an **FIP** to pick out the most important points: the ones you have you give priority and deal with first.

EXAMPLE

Someone wants to borrow some money from you. From the different factors, you pick out the following as being priorities:

Do you have the money?   Can you afford to lend it?
Do you trust the borrower?   When will the borrower pay it back?

PRACTICE

1. In doing a **CAF** on choosing a career, you may come up with the following factors: the pay; the chances of improvement or promotion; the people you would be working with; the work environment; the distance you would have to travel to get to work; the interest or enjoyment of the work. If you had to pick out the three top priorities from these factors, which would you choose?

PRACTICE (*continued*)

2. A father finds that his son has stolen a fishing rod from someone fishing in the canal. In dealing with the boy (aged 10) what should the father's priorities be?

3. Do an **AGO** on buying clothes and then do a **FIP** on the objectives you find.

4. In deciding whether you like someone or not, which factors do you think are the most important? Give the top three priorities.

5. If you were organizing a party, what would your priorities be?

★6. A nineteen-year-old boy wants to spend a year travelling around Africa. He asks his parents for some money. What should their priorities be in deciding whether to help him or not?

7. When people vote to elect a politician, what do you think their priorities should be? Do an **AGO** and list four priorities.

PROCESS

Discussion:

- Are priorities natural or should you make a special effort to choose them?
- Are the priorities always obvious?
- When is it most useful to find priorities?
- How do you choose priorities?

PRINCIPLES

A. It is important to get as many ideas as possible first and then to start picking out priorities.

B. Different people may have different priorities in the same situation.

C. You should know exactly why you have chosen something as a priority.

D. If it is difficult to choose the most important things, then try looking at it from the other direction: drop out the least important and see what you are left with.

E. The ideas not chosen as priorities must not be ignored. They too are considered – but after the priorities.

PROJECT

1. In running a school, what do you think the priorities should be?

2. What makes a TV program interesting. Do a **CAF** and then an **FIP**.

★3. If you were in charge of giving out money for research how would you choose to divide the money? What would your priorities be?

ISBN 0 08-034446-1

© 1986 Mica Management Resources (UK) Inc. All Rights Reserved. No part of this publication may be reproduced, stored in a retrieval system or transmitted in any form or by any means: electronic, electrostatic, magnetic tape, mechanical, photocopying, recording or otherwise, without permission in writing from the publishers.

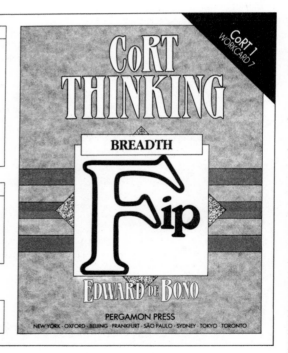

CoRT 1
WORKCARD 7

CoRT THINKING

BREADTH

Fip

EDWARD DE BONO

PERGAMON PRESS
NEW YORK · OXFORD · BEIJING · FRANKFURT · SÃO PAULO · SYDNEY · TOKYO · TORONTO

PRACTICE ITEM 2. Each group works on this problem for 4 minutes, at the end of which one group is designated to give its output. Other groups and individuals are then invited to say whether they agree with the designated group. This discussion must, however, be kept brief.

Suggestions:

- Getting the rod back to the person it belongs to.
- Pointing out to the boy why stealing is wrong.
- Trying to make sure it does not happen again.
- Being very angry.
- Punishing the boy.

PRACTICE ITEM 3. Each group does an **AGO** followed by a **FIP**. Time allowed is 3 minutes. One group is designated to give all the objectives. Another group then gives its top three priorities. The remaining groups can then disagree with these.

Suggestions:

AGO: to look nice, to be individual, to be in fashion, to keep warm, to spend as little money as possible, to compete with someone else.

FIP: to look nice, to keep warm, to spend as little money as possible.

PROCESS
(see Process section in inset of student workcard)

Open discussion with the class as a whole, acting as individuals rather than groups.

- Are priorities natural or should you make a special effort to choose them?
- Are the priorities always obvious?
- When is it most useful to find priorities?
- How do you choose priorities?

PRINCIPLES
*(see **Principles** section in inset of student workcard)*

The groups look at the list of principles given in the student workcards. They are asked to pick out the principle they think is most important. The groups can also be asked to criticize any one of the principles or to make up a principle of their own.

PROJECT
*(see **Project** section in inset of student workcard)*

When only a single period is allowed for the lesson there will not be time for this section. The project items can be used as essay topics or given to the students to work on in their own time. In longer lessons the group can work on a project item chosen by them or the teacher as described in the standard lesson format section.

HOW TO RUN
AN **APC** LESSON

APC: Alternatives, Possibilities, Choices

FOCUS ON ALTERNATIVES

> **APC** is a crystallization of the process of deliberately trying to find alternatives.

In taking action or making a decision, there may seem to be few alternatives, but a deliberate effort to find alternatives can change the whole situation. The **APC** operation is an attempt to focus attention directly on exploring all the alternatives or choices or possibilities – beyond the obvious ones.

In looking at a situation, it is unnatural to go beyond an explanation which seems satisfactory, and yet there may be other possibilities which may be even more likely if only an effort is made to find them. **The most likely alternative is not necessarily the most obvious.**

This deliberate search for alternatives applies not only to action but also to explanations. When an obvious explanation presents itself, it is very unnatural to look beyond it to try and find other possible explanations. That is why it is useful to have a device which can take one beyond natural inclinations.

The **APC** is an antidote to emotional reaction. Whenever a student seems to be looking at something in a rigid way, he/she can be asked to do an **APC**. If the student can do this then the result is either a change in view or an adherence to the original view, now however due to preference. **APC** can be applied to other subjects.

As in the **CAF** lesson, the emphasis in teaching is on what has been left out. That is to say, the groups try to find different alternatives and choices for the same situation to demonstrate that even when you are sure that there cannot be any other possibilities, you may still find some if you make a deliberate effort to look for them. As with the **CAF** lesson, it is all too easy to suppose that one naturally looks at all possible alternatives anyway – but it is not true. To go beyond the obvious and the satisfactory possibilities, one needs a deliberate device like the **APC**.

(see inset of student workcard for examples)

PRACTICE

*(see **Practice** section in inset of student workcard)*

Normally practice items 1, 2 and 3 are used one after the other. But for any one of these a teacher may choose to substitute practice items 4–7. Project items could also be used. The students work in groups as usual.

APC: ALTERNATIVES

APC = Alternatives, Possibilities, Choices

When you have to make a decision or take action, you may at first think that you do not have all the choices at your disposal. But if you look for them, you may find that there are more alternatives than you thought. Similarly in looking at a situation there are always obvious explanations. But if you look for them, you may find that there are other possible explanations that you had not thought of.

EXAMPLE

A car is found in a ditch and the driver is dead. What could have happened?

APC: The driver had a heart attack or fainted.
The car had a puncture, blow-out or mechanical failure.
The driver was drunk.
The driver misjudged the curve of the road.
The driver was attacked by a wasp and lost concentration.
The driver fell asleep.
The driver was murdered and then placed in the crashed car.

PRACTICE

★ 1. A man goes into a bar and asks for a drink of water. The woman behind the bar gives him a drink of water and then suddenly screams. What possible explanations are there?

2. You discover that your best friend is a thief. What alternatives do you have?

PRACTICE (continued)

★ 3. The Post Office is losing a lot of money. If you were running it, what alternatives would you have?

4. The brightest girl in class starts making mistakes in her work on purpose. What possible explanations are there?

★ 5. Fewer people want to be scientists. What possible explanations are there for this and what possible action can be taken?

6. Do an APC on all the different ways in which you could listen to rock music.

7. You want to get to sleep but a neighbor is playing very loud music. Do an APC on your alternatives. 1. What can you do right at the time? 2. What can you do to prevent it happening again?

PROCESS

Discussion:
● What is the point of looking for more alternatives?
● How do you tell which is the most likely or best alternative?
● When do you stop looking for other possibilities?
● When is it most useful to find new choices?

PRINCIPLES

A. If you cannot think of any alternatives yourself, you should ask someone else.

continued

PRINCIPLES (continued)

B. You go on looking for alternatives until you find one that you really like.

C. There is almost always an alternative, even if there does not appear to be one at first.

D. You cannot know that the obvious explanation is best until you have looked at some others.

E. To look for alternatives when you are not satisfied is easy but to look for them when you are satisfied requires a deliberate effort.

PROJECT

★ 1. A factory owner knows that if he pays the wages his workers demand and probably deserve he will lose money and will have to close the factory and then there will be unemployment in that area. What choices does he have?

2. A boy wants to get married but he has to stay at home to look after his aging father. What alternatives does he have?

★ 3. In dealing with pollution, what alternative courses of action are there?

ISBN 0 08-034446-1

© 1986 Mica Management Resources (UK) Inc. All Rights Reserved. No part of this publication may be reproduced, stored in a retrieval system or transmitted in any form or by any means: electronic, electrostatic, magnetic tape, mechanical, photocopying, recording or otherwise, without permission in writing from the publishers.

CoRT 1 WORKCARD 8

CoRT THINKING

BREADTH

APC
aPC
Apc
ApC
aPc
APc
apC
apc

EDWARD DE BONO

PERGAMON PRESS
NEW YORK · OXFORD · BEIJING · FRANKFURT · SÃO PAULO · SYDNEY · TOKYO · TORONTO

PRACTICE ITEM 1. Here, the groups are not allowed any actual thinking time. Instead, groups or individuals suggest possible explanations until someone hits on the suggestion given below. The other explanations can be listed. If no one guesses the explanation, the teacher can reveal this.

Suggestions of possible explanation:

- The man was hiccupping which is why he asked for a glass of water.
- The girl knew that hiccups were often cured by a sudden fright so she screamed to frighten the man.

PRACTICE ITEM 2. Groups work for 3 minutes on this. At the end of this time the teacher asks a group for the first alternative and then another group for another alternative until no more are forthcoming.

Suggestions:

- Tell him you know he is a thief.
- Report him.
- Threaten to report him.
- Drop him as a friend after telling him why.
- Drop him without telling him why.
- Say how much you hate stealing without saying that you know him to be a thief.
- Get someone else who is not a friend to talk to him.
- Leave a note in his desk, etc.

PRACTICE ITEM 3. Time allowed is 5 minutes. At the end of this time one group is designated to give its alternatives. Other groups and individuals are then invited to add to these one at a time.

Suggestions:

- Charge more for postage or telephones.
- Employ fewer people and have a slower delivery service.
- Introduce more automation.
- Make people collect their own letters from a central place.
- Charge more for certain types of mail such as business mail.
- Offer more money–making services.

PROCESS
*(see **Process** section in inset of student workcard)*

Open discussion with the class as a whole, acting as individuals rather than groups.

- What is the point of looking for more alternatives?
- How do you tell which is the most likely or best alternative?
- When do you stop looking for other possibilities?
- When is it most useful to find new choices?

PRINCIPLES
*(see **Principles** section in inset of student workcard)*

The groups look at the list of principles given in the student workcards. They are asked to pick out the principle they think is most important. The groups can also be asked to criticize any one of the principles or to make up a principle of their own.

PROJECT
*(see **Project** section inset of student workcard)*

When only a single period is allowed for the lesson there will not be time for this section. The project items can be used as essay topics or given to the students to work on in their own time. In longer lessons the groups can work on a project item chosen by themselves or the teacher as described in the standard lesson format section.

HOW TO RUN
A **DECISIONS** LESSON

DECISIONS

This lesson provides an opportunity to bring together the last two lessons in particular, **FIP** and **APC**, and also the other lessons in a more general way. In making decisions, you have to consider all the factors (**CAF**), be clear about aims and objectives (**AGO**), assess priorities (**FIP**), look at consequences (**C&S**) and discover the alternative courses that might be open (**APC**). You can also do a **PMI** on the decision once it has been made. The various aspects of thinking covered in the preceding lessons help to increase knowledge of the situation to the point where the decision either makes itself or is at least easier to make because the alternatives are more numerous and the consequences better defined.

In particular, the **FIP** process is important here. For instance, an **AGO** may turn up a number of different objectives for the decision, and then a deliberate **FIP** selects the most important. A **C&S** can then be done on the proposed decision and possibly a **PMI** as well. The lesson can be used to show the interplay of these different aspects of thinking.

As with previous lessons, no attempt is made to dictate values or rules for making decisions. The aim is to enlarge the view so that in reacting to the situation, the student has a broader view of it.

Once the decision situation is clarified, then a person responds to it in the usual manner using personal values.

PRACTICE
*(see **Practice** section in inset of student workcard)*

Normally practice items 1, 2 and 3 are used one after the other. The teacher may, however, choose to use practice items 4–7 or any of the project items instead. The students work in groups as usual.

PRACTICE ITEM 1. Each group works on the possible alternatives (**APC**). At the end of 3 minutes one group is designated to give the alternatives and the other groups can add to these. Then each group in turn is asked what decision they would make.

Suggestions:
- Stay where he is and radio for help.
- Try and get closer to see how many people are involved and if there is only one person, make an arrest.
- Radio for help, then go on in.
- Wait outside and then follow the person or people who came out.
- Find the getaway car and disable it.

DECISIONS

Some decisions are easy and some are difficult. There are decisions to be made all the time: which clothes to wear; which records to buy; whether to go out or not; how to amuse yourself; which career to choose; whether to stay on in a job or not; whether to go abroad; whether to spend money on something or to save it. Sometimes the decision is a choice between alternatives. Sometimes the decision is forced on you (e.g. when you come to a fork in the road and have to decide which road to take). In making decisions it is useful to be clear about factors involved (**CAF**), the objectives (**AGO**), the priorities (**FIP**), the consequences (**C&S**), and of course the alternatives (**APC**).

PRACTICE

1. A police officer notices a strange light in a warehouse at night. He is on his own and he has to make a quick decision as to what he is going to do.

2. A young man living at home with his widowed mother cannot find work in his own town but gets offered a job in another town quite far away. His mother says that she is too old to move and make new friends. He has to decide whether to take the job and leave his mother or refuse the job and stay at home.

★ 3. A girl has two boy friends: one of them is quiet and hardworking, the other is better looking and more fun but rather unreliable. Both want to marry her. She has to decide.

4. Parents with a crippled child have to decide whether to send her to a special school or to an ordinary school.

PRACTICE (continued)

★ 5. A politician has strong personal views about capital punishment. She is against such punishment. But she knows that the majority of her voters are in favor of capital punishment. When she has to give her opinion in the Senate on this matter, what should she do?

6. You are offered $100 now, or $200 in a year's time. How would you decide between the two? Explain the reasons behind your decisions. Do a **C&S** on both choices.

7. A friend of yours has quarrelled with the leader of the gang you hang out with. This friend has dropped out of the gang and wants you to drop out too. You have to decide whether to stay with the gang or not. How do you decide?

PROCESS

Discussion:

● Why are some decisions easier than others?

● What are the most important things to think about in making a decision?

● How can you tell that the decision you have made is the right one?

● Is it better to think about decisions or just to make them and see what happens?

PRINCIPLES

A. You should always be able to tell yourself the real reason behind any decision you make.

continued

PRINCIPLES (continued)

B. It is important to know whether a decision can be reversed or not after it has been made.

C. Not making a decision is really a decision to do nothing.

D. Decisions are very difficult to make if you are not prepared to give up something in order to gain something.

E. In making a decision, you should consider all the factors (**CAF**), look at the consequences (**C&S**), be very clear about objectives (**AGO**), assess the priorities (**FIP**), and find all the possible alternatives (**APC**). When you have done this, a decision may be much easier.

PROJECT

★ 1. The head of a big business is kidnapped, and the kidnappers demand a large amount of money for his release. The police know that if the money is given, then other people will be kidnapped for money. If the money is not given, the man will be killed. How should the decision be made?

★ 2. A state housing officer knows that if he does a lot to find homes for the homeless in his area then homeless people in other areas will hear of this and move into his area and the problem will never be solved. What can he decide?

3. How do people decide to spend their money?

ISBN 0 08-034446-1

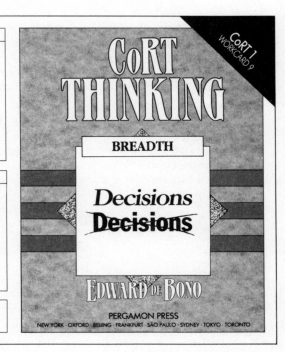

CoRT 1 WORKCARD 9

CoRT THINKING

BREADTH

Decisions Decisions

EDWARD de BONO

PERGAMON PRESS
NEW YORK · OXFORD · BEIJING · FRANKFURT · SÃO PAULO · SYDNEY · TOKYO · TORONTO

PRACTICE ITEM 2. One group is asked to do priorities (**FIP**); another group is asked to do consequences for both decisions (**C&S**); another group does objectives (**AGO**); and another looks for alternatives (**APC**). Each group also makes a decision. At the end of 3 minutes one group is designated for each of the above procedures and every group is asked for its decision.

Suggestions:

FIP: Money for both himself and his mother to live on.
           The likelihood of getting a job in his own town.

C&S: If he does go away his mother may adjust to living on her own, especially if he is sending her money.
           If he stays at home he is going to be so frustrated that he will take it out on his mother.

AGO: The happiness of his mother and himself.
           Providing the circumstances for that happiness.
           To get a permanent job.

APC: His mother comes with him for a short while to see how she likes it.
           He commutes or comes home on weekends.
           He sets a deadline of 3 months to see if he can find work locally.
           He gives it a try for 3 months to see how his mother gets on.

PRACTICE ITEM 3. Time allowed is 3 minutes. In this case half the class is told that the girl has decided to marry the quiet fellow and the other half that she has decided to marry the fun fellow. Each group has to try to imagine the reasons behind the decision they are given. One group is then designated to support each decision.

Suggestions:

Quiet boyfriend
- Fun boyfriends are alright for fun, but they may want to go on having fun and leave you.
- Reliability is more important for a long-term partner.
- She found out that the fun boyfriend had another girl friend.

Fun boyfriend
- Life is not worth living if you are bored, but if you are having a good time you can put up with anything.
- The fun boyfriend might settle down and be reliable.
- Her parents oppose him.
- She could always try it for a while.
- You only live once.

PROCESS
*(see **Process** section in inset of student workcard)*

Open discussion with the class as a whole, acting as individuals rather than groups.

- Why are some decisions easier than others?
- What are the most important things to think about in making a decision?
- How can you tell that the decision you have made is the right one?
- Is it better to think about decisions or just to make them and see what happens?

PRINCIPLES

*(see **Principles** section in inset of student workcard)*

The groups look at the list of principles given in the student workcards. They are asked to pick out the principle they think is most important. The group can also be asked to criticize any one of the principles or to make up a principle of their own.

PROJECT

*(see **Project** section in inset of student workcard)*

When only a single period is allowed for the lesson there will not be time for this section. The project items can be used as essay subjects or given to the students for them to work on in their own time. In longer lessons the groups can work on a project item chosen by the teacher as described in the standard lesson format section.

HOW TO RUN
AN **OPV** LESSON

OPV: Other People's Views

THE OTHER PEOPLE INVOLVED

OPV is a crystallization of the process of looking at other people's viewpoints so that the process can be used consciously and deliberately.

In the preceding nine lessons, the enlargement of the situation – the broadening of perception – has always been from the point of view of the thinker. But many thinking situations involve other people as well. The point of view of these other people is also an essential part of the enlargement of the situation which is the basic theme of these first ten lessons. Thus, another person may have different objectives, different priorities, different alternatives, etc. In fact, when another person does a **PMI**, **CAF**, **C&S**, **AGO**, **FIP** or **APC**, he or she may come up with different ideas because he or she is in a different position.

Being able to look at and understand another person's point of view may be a very important part indeed of the thinking process, and so a deliberate effort may have to be made to see another point of view. This deliberate effort is the **OPV**. It may apply to another person's point of view or to other people's points of view in general.

Like many of the previous operations, **OPV** as a tool can be applied in different subject areas. It may be applied by itself, or it may be applied in conjunction with another operation. "Do an **OPV-AGO** for the other person."

Once students can escape from their own points of view, they can take other people into consideration. They may even come up with useful new ways of looking at a situation.

The **OPV** is an antidote to selfishness. Instead of a general vague feeling that other peoples' points of view matter, **there is a deliberate attempt to see another person's point of view**.

In teaching, the emphasis must be on how the view of another person in the same situation may be entirely different. It is the possible difference between points of view that matters here. If it is assumed that any sensible person would have the same point of view in a given situation, then no effort at all will be made to see other points of view.

PRACTICE
*(see **Practice** section in inset of student workcard)*

Normally practice items 1, 2 and 3 are used one after the other. But for any one of these a teacher may choose to substitute practice items 4–7 or any of the project items. The students work in groups.

OPV: OTHER PEOPLE'S VIEWS

OPV = Other People's Views

Many thinking situations involve other people. What these other people think is just as much part of the situation as the factors, the consequences, the objectives, etc. These other people may have a very different viewpoint. Although they are in the same situation, they may look at things very differently. It is a very important part of thinking to be able to tell how other people are thinking; trying to see things from another person's viewpoint is what doing an **OPV** is about. Another person may consider different factors (**CAF**), see different consequences (**C&S**), have different objectives (**AGO**) or priorities (**FIP**). In fact, all the thinking that you do for yourself, others may be doing for themselves — but differently.

EXAMPLE

A salesperson is trying to sell you a used sports car. The salesperson's point of view is to show how sharp it is, how powerful the engine, the new tires, how it suits you, what a good buy it is. Your point of view is to see whether it has been in a crash, how much spare tires cost, how worn the parts are, how much gas it uses, how it compares to other cars you have seen.

PRACTICE

1. A father forbids his daughter of 13 to smoke. What is his point of view and what is hers?

2. An inventor discovers a new way of making cloth. This invention means that only one person out of every twenty would still be employed in making cloth. Do an **OPV** for the inventor, the factory owner, the workers, and the general public.

PRACTICE (*continued*)

★ 3. A next-door neighbor opens her home as a refuge for sick people who have no one to care for them. Some neighbors object very strongly and some do not mind. What are the points of view of the refuge owner, the people using the refuge, those who object, and those who do not mind?

4. There is a train strike and people find it difficult to get to work. How many different points of view are involved in this situation?

5. A boy refuses to obey his teacher in class. The teacher reports the boy to the principal who suspends him. The boy's parents object. What are the viewpoints of the boy, the teacher, the principal, the parents, his classmates?

6. Do an **OPV** on someone who has just realized he is on the wrong airplane, going to the wrong city.

7. There is a minor traffic accident. The drivers start shouting at each other and eventually start fighting. Do an **OPV** for each driver.

PROCESS

Discussion:

- Is it easy to see other viewpoints?
- Whose point of view is right if two points of view differ?
- If other people cannot see your point of view, should you bother about theirs?
- Why is it necessary to see someone else's viewpoint?
- Should your action be based on your own viewpoint or someone else's as well?

PRINCIPLES

A. You ought to be able to see the other point of view whether you agree with it or not.

B. Every point of view may be right for the person holding it but not right enough to be imposed on others.

C. Different people have different positions, backgrounds, knowledge, interests, values, wants, etc., so it is not surprising that in the same situation viewpoints may differ greatly.

D. Try to see whether the other person can see your viewpoint.

E. Be able to articulate the differences and similarities between viewpoints.

PROJECT

★ 1. A lawyer is defending in court a man whom he believes to be guilty of stealing some money. What are the viewpoints of the lawyer, the judge, the accused man and the jury?

2. There is a plan to pull down some old houses and build modern apartments with wider roads in between them. What are the viewpoints of the planners, the architects, and the adults and children who live in the houses?

★ 3. Many people talk about pollution, but cleaning up the environment costs money. What are the viewpoints of an ordinary citizen, an environmental group, industrialists, the government?

ISBN 0 08-034446-1

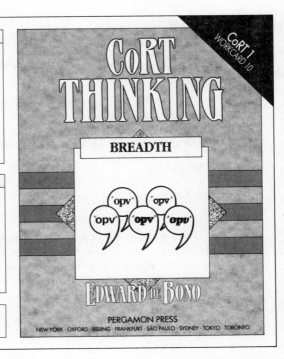

CoRT 1
WORKCARD 10

CoRT THINKING

BREADTH

EDWARD DE BONO

PERGAMON PRESS
NEW YORK · OXFORD · BEIJING · FRANKFURT · SÃO PAULO · SYDNEY · TOKYO · TORONTO

PRACTICE ITEM 1. Each group works on both points of view for 3 minutes. At the end of this time one group is designated to give the father's point of view and another group is designated to give the girl's. Other groups and individuals can then add to these as usual.

Suggestions:

Girl
- She only wants to try it out, all her friends smoke and she does not want to appear afraid.
- She wants to be able to make decisions for herself; sooner or later she will be able to smoke if she wants to.
- She cannot see any harm in it.

Father
- It is bad for health.
- It wastes money.
- She would smell awful.
- It shows that he is not bringing her up properly.
- She is too young to think for herself as an adult.

PRACTICE ITEM 2. One group is selected for each of the categories (or more than one group if necessary). They work on the item for three minutes. Then a group is designated to give each of the outputs.

Suggestions:

Inventor
- The joy of invention and seeing it work.
- Wants to get it into use as quickly as possible.
- Money from royalties.

The factory owner
- Bigger profits.
- Less trouble with labor.
- Can produce much more and compete with countries where labor is cheaper.

The workers
- Losing a job for the sake of someone else's profits.
- No other jobs in the area.
- Would need training for other jobs.
- Do not mind invention as long as their jobs are secure.

The general public
- If cloth were cheaper, clothing would be cheaper to buy so they are in favor if invention lowers prices.

PRACTICE ITEM 3. After 1 minute's preparation each group is asked to play the role of one of the categories. They may be allowed to choose these roles but the unchosen roles get distributed. One group only for each role. Then the role groups in turn give their assumed point of view. The other groups can comment but an argument or general discussion is not intended.

Suggestions:

The refuge owner
- It is her house and she wants to do something to help people.
- The least contribution those around can make is to keep quiet.

The people using the refuge
- At a time of need and desperation it is a very welcome place to go.
- Those who are fortunate should not object.

Those who object
- There are proper places for refugees which should not be placed in a quiet residential district.
- There might be disease brought in.
- The children might be upset.
- The welfare system makes proper provision for such people.
- Such people should have worked harder when they could.

Those who do not mind
- It is the owner's business what she does with her house.
- It is good to help the unfortunate.
- There is no real disruption.
- Children should learn about another side of life.

PROCESS
*(see **Process** section in inset of student workcard)*

Open discussion with the class as a whole, acting as individuals rather than groups.

- Is it easy to see other viewpoints?
- Whose point of view is right if two points of view differ?
- If other people cannot see your point of view should you bother about theirs?
- Why is it necessary to see someone else's viewpoint?
- Should your action be based on your own viewpoint or someone else's as well?

PRINCIPLES
*(see **Principles** section in inset of student workcard)*

The groups look at the list of principles given in the student workcards. They are asked to pick out the principle they think is most important. The groups can also be asked to criticize any one of the principles, or to make up a principle of their own.

PROJECT
*(see **Project** section in inset of student workcard)*

When only a single period is allowed for the lessons there will not be time for this section. The project items can be used as essay topics or given to the students to work on in their own time. In longer lessons the groups can work on a project item chosen by them or the teacher as described in the standard lesson format section.

TEACHING METHOD

The structure of thinking lessons and the way they are conducted will be considered under the following four headings:

GROUPS
NOTES
TIME
THE TEACHER

GROUPS

In the **CoRT** Thinking Lessons the students work in groups. This group format is very basic to the lessons for several reasons. If the students work as individuals then the brighter students tend to give all the answers or become impatient if they are not allowed to do so. The other students do not get involved at all since they are unable to see the thinking that leads to the answer.

In the group situation even the dullest and most silent member of the group can watch in action the thinking of the more able group members as they discuss matters. The timidity and shyness that prevent many students from offering opinions disappear when they are operating within their own small groups instead of with the teacher and the whole class. Within each group there is much more time for back-and-forth discussion, disagreement and alternative points of view than there could ever be with the whole class, since the members of each group can talk more often. Finally, the very nature of the thinking lessons involves the practice of a particular thinking operation and this is easiest in small groups. It is **not** a matter of receiving knowledge or finding the right answer.

In several schools the thinking lessons have provided the only opportunity for the students to work in groups and this in itself can have a socializing value. The students themselves seem to enjoy working in groups.

Forming the Groups

There are several ways of doing this:

1. Groups put together by the teacher who knows the class and divides it into the groups that would work best.

2. Arbitrary arrangement according to where students are sitting. This can also be done by having the students pick up slips of paper which assign them to a particular group.

3. The teacher can choose group leaders who then pick their own groups.

4. Natural groups in which a group of friends work together.

The grouping of friends is not recommended since they may find their own company so delightful that little attention is paid to the lesson itself. With a very well-motivated class, however, the method can work.

Size of Groups

This depends very much on the nature of the class. For instance a remedial group of nine children would operate best as a single group with the children clustered around the teacher. On the other hand very articulate high-achieving students can feel very frustrated in large groups since their individual ideas cannot get through. In this case a group size of five would be best.

The way the teacher chooses to run the lesson can also affect group size. For instance, if the teacher wants a full output from each group then more than four groups are impractical because of the time involved. If, however, only one group is designated to give a full output and the other groups simply add extra suggestions then a large number of small groups becomes possible. In this case each group acts as an individual might in an ordinary class. In general, the more articulate the students the smaller the group size has to be. On the other hand small groups which do not produce much output can be re-grouped into larger groups. The ideal group size is four. More than six is difficult and over eight is impossible.

Spokesperson

There are times when someone has to give the outlook of the whole group. This spokesperson should be determined beforehand. The spokesperson may want to take down in note form the output produced by the group. There is no need to have a formal chairperson or leader unless the group is so large that a chairperson is needed to see that everyone does not speak at once. From time to time the teacher may call upon a different member of the group to be spokesperson in order to give everyone a chance to express the ideas of the group. But there is little point in forcing a reluctant student to do this.

Change of Groups

The groups may be changed from time to time: for instance after every three lessons. If the students want to change more frequently or less frequently this can be done. Minor switches can be made if there are personality difficulties or if a teacher notices that a particular group is very weak. Sometimes one or two individuals want to opt out of a group to work on their own. This should not be encouraged but may be allowed in exceptional circumstances.

Disadvantages of Groups

Some high-achieving students find that in a group they cannot express their own ideas because of the necessity for compromise and in any case the ideas are credited to the group rather than themselves. In fact in the lessons there are opportunities for individuals to respond on their own either in the discussion period or in the offering of additional ideas after the designated group has given its output. With these high-achieving students it is worth using the individual test material from time to time. With this material they can operate on their own as individuals.

Group Output

The members of a group discuss the situation they have been asked to think about and develop their ideas and conclusions. One of the groups is then designated by the teacher to give its output through its spokesperson. The other groups listen and can then add their own ideas, comments or disagreements provided that they are new points. These additions may be done either by the group spokesperson or by individuals in a group. If they have something to say the groups try to attract the teacher's attention and the teacher chooses the desired groups.

There are other ways to organize the output. For instance in some cases each group in turn gives one point. In some cases the groups are tackling different situations and here each group has to give its own output. The output is usually verbal but the teacher can also ask for an output in note form if the groups are being lazy. The way in which the teacher handles long-winded or facetious outputs is dealt with in the section describing the teacher's role on page 47.

NOTES

For each lesson there are teacher's notes and student workcards. A set of student workcards is given to each student at the beginning of each lesson. It is important that the students keep their workcards since they contain the essential principles of the lesson in addition to the practice material. In this way students gradually assemble their own textbooks.

Structure

Each lesson has the same basic structure just as each meal has the same basic structure given by the different courses. Within this structure the content varies widely.

Each of the thinking lessons consists of the following basic sections:

Introduction: explains the particular aspect of thinking covered in that lesson and gives an example.

Practice: provides problems and situations for the practice of thinking.

Process: opens class discussion of the aspect of thinking that is the subject of that lesson.

Principles: gives five basic principles concerning the subject of the lesson for the groups to examine and comment on.

Project: provides further problems and thinking situations which can be tackled at the time or later. The full nature of these sections and variations in the arrangement of them will be discussed later.

Where the lessons are used with students who might have difficulty in reading the notes, the teacher can read out the separate items to the class.

Resources

The only resources used are those already present in the minds of the students. **Thinking is the skilled use of already available information.** The students are not required to absorb film strips, books or other material before they can start thinking. The notes serve only to trigger the student's minds. That is why the same notes can be used with such a wide range of student ages and abilities. In each case the trigger is the same though what is triggered may be very different.

Since the students are not required to absorb material before they can begin to think those students who are not good at absorbing material on account of disability or inattention find that they can function well in thinking lessons.

Content

Each lesson contains a variety of problems and thinking situations. Since it is impossible to predict the interest of every teacher or class there is a wide mix of material. Some of it is directly relevant to a student's own world and experience. Some of it is deliberately remote so that a student can practice thinking objectively. Some of it is designed to encourage students to think about situations they might usually regard as outside their competence.

The variation in content is very important, for the purpose of the thinking lessons is to direct attention to the process. This can happen only if there is sufficient variation in the content so that no single item occupies too much time. In this way students are forced to shift their attention from the content to the process. This point is fundamental. If the lesson becomes a discussion on one of the practice items, it may be fascinating but it becomes useless as a thinking lesson.

It is not easy to predict what content will interest a particular class. For instance, one class of nine-year-olds became very interested in the problem of whether parents should send a crippled child to a special school or an ordinary one. Another class was fascinated by the science fiction suggestion of a breakfast pill that would replace food. Social realism and problems immediately related to the students' world are not necessarily the ones that most interest the students, though an attempt should be made to include a fair proportion of these.

In each lesson, teachers may choose from a selection of alternative practice items to find the ones suited to their classes. For instance, a class of nine-year-olds may not be interested in environmental problems.

Teachers who do not like the given practice items may invent their own, providing they relate to the purpose of the lesson.

It cannot be emphasized often enough that the **purpose of the lessons is to develop thinking as a skill that can be applied to any situation.** The purpose is not to have general discussions on interesting topics.

TIME

The lessons are designed to be used **once a week for 10 weeks**. *A greater frequency is not advisable.* Any extra lesson periods may be used for the test material. The lessons are designed to be used with a minimal lesson time of 35 minutes or with longer periods up to twice the minimum.

With 35-minute lessons the practice section may have to be shortened and the project section usually omitted. With longer periods it is possible to extend the practice section both by allowing more time per item and by using more items; the discussion period would be longer and the project section could be tackled.

The introductory set of 10 lessons is part of a two-year syllabus of 60 lessons covering different aspects of thinking.

THE TEACHER

The teacher's role will vary with the age and ability of the students, the type of class and the motivation involved. For instance a high-achieving sixth grade group (aged 12–13) used to working in a tightly structured situation with right answers for which they get individual credit will need a different sort of approach than a class of 10-year-olds bubbling with ideas for the sheer joy of it.

The teacher's role may be considered under the following headings:

Choice
Variation
Enrichment
Control
Emphasis
Response
Achievement

Choice

The teacher may choose the order in which to do the different sections in the lesson. Various alternatives are outlined in the section on alternatives (see page 55) and teachers may also generate their own. Teachers choose which practice items would be suited to their classes or again may generate their own. Teachers choose the type of output wanted from the groups. Teachers also choose how they are going to set up the groups, how much time is going to be given to each item, and when they are going to use test material if they think this is appropriate. Teachers also choose which group will give its output and from which other groups to accept additional suggestions. In fact, the lessons can be adapted to suit any particular teaching situation.

Variation

Apart from the specific variations suggested in the Alternatives section and elsewhere in these notes, the teacher can choose to inject different variations so long as the essential purpose of the lesson is not destroyed. For instance, the teacher may decide to try one of the practice items with a role-playing or debate format or as a scoring game.

To relieve the sameness of the lessons, teachers are encouraged to introduce as much variation as they wish, relying on their own teaching experience and knowledge of the class. Nevertheless, it must be remembered that the purpose of any lesson is to focus on a particular aspect of thinking. A general discussion on some topic is unlikely to serve this purpose.

Enrichment

These notes only provide a bare skeleton to be fleshed out. The interest of the lessons depends on the teacher's ability to enrich the items suggested in the notes. In setting one of the practice problems, a teacher should build up the situation into an interesting one rather than just asking the students to tackle item number 3 in their notes.

For instance in the **C&S** lesson, one item concerns a robot that is developed to replace human labor in factories. The teacher could paint the scene in terms of the empty factories with only a few workers in white coats to look after the robots. In the **AGO** lesson students are asked to consider objectives of a homemaker, shop-keeper, food manufacturer and farmer with regard to food. The teacher can set the scene in terms of the homemaker on his own, the shop-keeper working for herself or for a supermarket chain (and give it local identity if possible), the manufacturer in terms of a specific name and the farmer growing crops.

Enrichment also refers to the explanation of the thinking process that is the subject of the lesson. More or better examples can be given here.

Finally, enrichment refers to the way the teacher deals with the output from the groups. Teachers can comment and elaborate on ideas that are put forward. They can link one idea with another or contrast them. Teachers do not have to accept passively the ideas that are offered. They can work on them and develop the interest in them.

Control

This is important. The lessons should run at a fast pace. The overall aim should be one of crispness and effectiveness. Without this the lessons can easily degenerate into aimless drifting. To maintain the crispness the teacher must be in control. If control is lost the lessons can tend to flop into purposelessness. In the thinking lessons the teacher does not have the authority of imparting superior knowledge but still retains the controlling initiative. The teacher can comment on ideas or cut off a discussion and move on to the next item when they want to. The teacher can choose to ask any group or individual for a comment or choose not to.

The degree to which teachers may have to exercise control will vary with the class. With a well-motivated class teachers may simply be caretakers watching the thinking as it flows. With a more difficult class they may have to be quite tough until the class gets into the swing of the lessons. Students used to structure and control may take some time to adjust to thinking lessons.

The four most difficult situations are as follows:

facetiousness: Teachers may have their own way of dealing with this. Silly remarks can be treated as such and groups which persist in making them can be ignored. The composition of a group can be changed. The teacher must, however, be sure that it is really facetiousness and not a genuine attempt at an unusual point of view.

wordiness: This can be a difficulty with some groups and some items. The teacher can ask a person or group to summarize the three main points of what is to be said. The teacher can also cut off a discussion and move on. If students feel they are not getting enough time, then the written output of the test material can be used.

silence: It may be difficult to generate ideas. If no ideas are forthcoming, teachers should make suggestions of their own for the students to react to. The teacher's notes for each lesson usually contain suggestions for this purpose.

laziness: A particular group may decide to let all the other groups do the work. Such a group can be designated by the teacher as the one required to give its output to the rest of the class. Output in note form can also be requested and these can be compared by the teacher.

Emphasis

It is entirely up to teachers to keep the central purpose of the lesson in front of the class. It is very easy for the lesson to drift into a general discussion of some topic. When this happens teachers must repeatedly focus attention on the actual thinking process that is the subject of the lesson. They should not be shy about using the labels and should be able to ask someone to do a **PMI** on an idea or a **CAF** on some situation. Though these will sound artificial at first, this soon passes.

It is also up to teachers to emphasize the difference between the different thinking operations. If all the lessons deal directly with content, then they are all going to seem alike since the content is not particular to any lesson. Teachers must point out the difference between **APC** and **AGO** and between **C&S** and **CAF**, etc. This can be done in the initial introduction period or during the open discussion.

Response

Many teachers make the mistake of assuming that since there is no one right answer in the thinking lessons, they cannot judge the ideas offered but must accept them all. There is no one right answer but there are many possible right answers.

There are many wrong answers, silly answers or trivial answers, and the teacher is perfectly justified in treating them as such. The only thing that teachers must not do is to dismiss an idea simply because it differs from their own. Quite apart from the right/wrong basis of judgment, there are many other ways in which a teacher can comment on a suggestion. In fact, since the right/wrong basis is inappropriate, there is an increased opportunity to use other modes.

Some possible responses are listed below.

- How is that idea different from the one we just had?
- Could you compare your idea with the other one?
- Is that an important idea or just an idea?
- Which of the two do you think is more important?
- I cannot understand what you mean – could you explain further?
- What would happen then – what is the point of that?
- Why do you think this is a new idea which we have not had yet?
- Could you condense all those variations into a single idea?
- That is a silly idea.
- That is not very important, is it?
- What else can you think of in that connection?
- Do you have anything to add to that idea?
- Do you agree with the idea we have just heard?

Achievement

This can be a difficult point, especially for those students who have been used to dealing with situations for which there are definite right answers. They miss the sense of achievement and personal credit. They are also unsure of the rules of the thinking lessons and what they are aiming for. It is up to the teacher to create a sense of achievement. This is not based on the right answer system but on **having something to say, on having some thoughts on the matter**. For instance the teacher can acclaim an idea in the following matter:

- That is a very important point.
- We have not had that point before.
- That is a very interesting idea (a new angle).
- That is a very original idea indeed.
- That is a very interesting variation of the idea we have already had.
- That is a neat (or elegant) idea.

Similarly, a group output can be praised in the above way or as follows:

- That is a very well organized output.
- Those ideas are very comprehensive.
- That is very imaginative.
- I do not think there will be much to add.
- You have covered most points.
- That is very competent.

Expressing displeasure is rather more difficult because it depends not so much on the idea itself but on the teacher's assessment of the motivation involved. **The teacher is not really judging ideas but judging whether the students are practicing thinking.** There is no point in condemning the output of someone who is genuinely trying. On the other hand, someone who is being facetious or lazy can be treated with the following remarks instead of bland acceptance:

- That is rather silly.
- That is a weak idea.
- I am sure that you can do better than that.
- We have already had that idea.
- That idea is exactly the same as the other one.

Similarly a group output can be treated as follows:

- You have left out a great deal.
- I do not think you have coped with that problem.
- That is all very superficial and obvious.
- You must try harder than that.

In general, the thinking lessons are not different from lessons in other subjects which do not have absolute answers – for instance, English.

The main points to remember are:

1. If students are really trying their hardest, you cannot get them to think better by condemning their performances.

2. If students are lazy or facetious then their output can be judged on its face value.

3. There are many ways of praising an idea apart from saying it is the only right idea.

4. A distinction has to be made between trivial and important ideas if there seems to be deliberate generation of trivial ideas.

SUMMARY

The main points are that the teacher should:

- Make the lessons interesting.
- Maintain control and a brisk pace.
- Keep the focus on the process rather than the content.
- Give the students a definite sense of achievement.

STANDARD LESSON FORMAT

The standard lesson format is given below. Some variations will be discussed in connection with the use of the lessons by students of different age and ability (see pages 69-73). Some alternative formats are also given at the end of this section and other variations are given in the section itself. Teachers are encouraged to develop their own variations.

INTRODUCTION

Both the teacher's notes and the student workcards contain an explanatory introduction which explains very briefly the aspect of thinking that is the subject of the lesson. There is no need for the teacher to read this out unless the students have difficulty in reading. Teachers can give a brief explanation centered on the examples that are given in the student workcards and sometimes in the teacher's notes as well. Teachers can add further examples or alter the ones given as wished. This explanation must be brief because time is short, and in any case a much fuller discussion takes place in the process section of the lessons. The students can be left to read the introduction in their own workcards for themselves whenever they like during the lesson.

PRACTICE

Item

Each lesson contains five practice items. These items provide a direct opportunity for the students to practice the thinking operation which is the basis of the lesson. Normally, the teacher would use items 1, 2, and 3 in order, but items 4–7 are provided specifically for any teachers who feel that they may be more suited to their own class. In that case, these alternative items can be used instead of any of the others. Teachers may also alter the order of the items. If they wish, they can borrow items from the project section, invent some of their own and use some suggested by the students themselves.

The practice items are presented verbally to the class by the teachers who elaborate and enrich the item as they do so. It is up to the teachers to give the item the setting and specificity which they feel would be most suitable for their class. For instance, a general item can be put in terms specific to a particular neighborhood.

The students then begin working on the item. They work in groups as has been discussed earlier. It is suggested that one member of the group take notes regarding the group's conclusions. This person may also serve as spokesperson who will eventually represent the group's conclusions before the class.

Completion time for each item varies from 1–5 minutes and is visually indicated in the teacher's notes. This tends to be on the short side, and in exceptional cases more time may be allowed. However, there is little time allotted for each lesson, and the emphasis should be on speed. When more time is allowed for the lesson, the time spent on each practice item may be increased, but boredom should never be permitted to prevail.

Output

The output from the groups is usually verbal. If teachers find that the groups are having difficulty in expressing their ideas verbally, output in writing may also be used.

With many of the practice items each group is working on the same problem. In this case one of the groups is designated to give its output to the whole class. This group is referred to in these notes as the designated group. The designated group gives a full output. Any other group or individual can then add additional points left out by the designated group by attracting the teacher's attention. This continues until no further points are forthcoming. If a point offered is not really a new point but only a minor variation of one already given, the teacher should say so in order to discourage this sort of thing. Comments may also be allowed if there is time, but arguments waste too much time. The teacher may also ask questions of a group as a whole or of individuals within a group. No one knows which group is going to be designated to give its output until after the practice item has been considered. Normally, the teacher should try to maintain a sort of random rotation so that each group would be designated sooner or later. But if one group is particularly lazy and never seems to contribute anything, that group can be called upon more frequently. Similarly, if a particular group is being sarcastic, the teacher can ignore that group for a while. Designated groups could also be chosen by putting slips bearing a group name into a container and then drawing one at random.

In some of the practice items, the groups work on different problems or different aspects of the same problem. In that case, the teacher tells each group which problem or part of the problem it is to work on. The others can add further ideas as usual. If there are many groups there may be more than one group working on the same part.

In other cases, the teacher may go around the groups one by one asking for a single point from each group until no more new points are forthcoming.

Sometimes the groups are asked to produce as many ideas as they can in a fixed period of time. At the end of this time, the group which claims the largest number of ideas is allowed to be the designated group.

In general, the teacher can treat groups as if they were individuals in the matter of asking for outputs.

Suggestions

These suggestions are intended to supplement the teacher's own ideas on a problem, so that more ideas will be available if necessary. They are not intended as right answers. If the group's output does not include these suggestions, teachers may point them out.

Occasionally, some of the practice items have suggested answers which the groups are supposed to include among their other suggestions. The point here is not that these are right answers, but that any full consideration of the subject can be reasonably expected to include these answers. This particular use of the suggestions would be indicated in the notes.

Number of Items

The number of practice items tackled is determined by the total time available for the lesson and also by the time taken for the groups to report their output. Ideally, **each lesson should try to cover three practice items**, but sometimes this may have to be reduced to two. The teacher must, however, try to prevent the lesson from becoming a long discussion and argument about the content of one of the practice items. The emphasis must always be kept focused on the thinking operation that is the subject of the lesson. This is why it is necessary to have a variety of practice items even if there is not enough time to consider each one thoroughly. **A brisk pace is essential.**

PROCESS

The process discussion section provides an opportunity for the teacher to discuss with the class as a whole the thinking process that is the subject of the lesson. The students remain in their groups but can operate as individuals. There is no group discussion in this section. All discussion is between the teacher and students or between student and student in front of the whole class. The teacher can ask questions of individuals and take comments from them without going through the group structure.

For each lesson, the teacher's notes contain suggestions as to the sort of questions that might be used in the process discussion section. These same questions are also given in the student workcards. There is no need to stick to them and certainly no need to go through them one by one. There are questions about the nature of the process, the need for it, the difficulty in using it, what happens if it is used, whether it is natural or needs to be used deliberately and so on. The discussion should, however, be operated as a normal discussion and if some interesting points come up they can be pursued. The pace of the process discussion should be crisp and brisk, and the discussion as a whole should take 5 or 10 minutes at the most.

In an alternative way of running the lesson, the principle section and the process section can be run together so that the discussion can also take in the principles as something to be discussed. Teachers can try this as a variation and see if it works better.

PRINCIPLES

Each set of lesson notes contains five principles listed for each of the lessons. The principles are not meant to be dogmatic points. They are intended to draw the lesson together and to say specific things about that aspect of thinking which is the subject of the lesson. They are also intended as a focal point for the organization of the students' thoughts on the subject. There is nothing absolute about the particular principles chosen.

The groups look at the list of principles and then do one or more of the following things:

1. Pick out the principle they feel to be most important.
2. Comment upon or criticize any particular one of the principles.
3. Add a new principle of their own.

The older groups can be asked to do all or any one of these things. With younger groups, it is enough if they pick out the principle they judge to be the most important. Teachers ask each group in turn, and if there is any difference of opinion this can be discussed or commented upon by the group concerned. For instance one group may want to explain to all the other groups why it has chosen a different principle.

Time allowed for this section is 3–5 minutes. The important point is not what the groups choose, but that in order to choose they have to look at each of the principles and develop some thoughts about them. This is the essential purpose of the principles section.

Since the students are meant to keep their workcards, the principles section also acts as a summary of the whole lesson for future reference.

PROJECT

In a single lesson of 35 minutes, it is very unlikely that there will be any time at all for this project section. In that case it can be ignored. Those schools which are used to giving project work for students to work on outside the classroom can use the project items in this way. Alternatively, the project items can become the subject for essays or discussion sessions.

Where the lesson is long enough, the teacher or the groups themselves decide which project item is to be worked on. It is best if the groups all work on the same item because a general discussion is then possible afterwards. The groups spend up to 15 minutes working on the item. The teacher moves around from group to group watching the group thinking and even taking part. At the end of this time, each group gives its output to the class and discussion can also take place. Alternatively, there can be a written output in note form from the groups.

Project items can also be transferred to the practice section and used as practice items if the teacher wishes.

ALTERNATIVES

A number of variations can be made in the standard lesson format and some of these are outlined below. Teachers can also use their own variation provided the basic points of the lesson are not lost.

Practice Session

Some teachers prefer to give only one practice item after the introduction. After this they move directly to the process discussion and principles. They then return to do one or more of the practice items as time allows. This is a good variation. But care must be taken that the process discussion does not take up the whole of the lesson. Practicing the thinking operation is more important than talking about it. However, the students may practice the operation before and after discussing it and allow time for completion of the final practice items.

With younger children and especially with remedial groups, there is no need for a separate process and principles section. The lesson consists of practice items which are worked upon either by groups or, if the whole class is very small, by a single class group. The process discussion and principles are woven into the discussion that follows the output from the groups. This variation relies very much on the teacher's control of the class and certainty that the process is actually discussed.

Principles and Process Discussion

In classes that are not very articulate, it may help to put the principles section before the process section or at least treat them together. In this way the process discussion can center on the principles as well as the suggested questions. Another way to operate these sections is to have some discussion, then to look at the principles, and then to continue the discussion.

One advantage of this method is that the lesson ends with the discussion rather than the selection of principles. This means that the discussion can be lengthened or compressed according to how much time is left.

Follow-up Lesson

Ideally, each thinking lesson should occupy a double period. Sometimes it is possible to use two single periods a week. In this case, the ordinary lesson is done in the first session but one of the practice items can be omitted. In the second session a brief summary is given of what was done in the first session and then the groups set to work on a project item. They can work either as groups or as individuals doing the item as an essay. One or two items are used depending on the nature of the item. During group work, the teacher moves around from group to group and can take part in the group discussion. With essay work, the written material can be collected at the end of the session and commented on as with an ordinary essay. Comments should of course refer to the thinking content rather than the style. A period is set aside at the end of lesson, whether the output is group or individual, for discussion of the conclusions reached. In this discussion the teacher must try and bring out the process involved since this will usually be well hidden within the content.

Timing

The timing for two possible variations of the lesson could be as follows:

I	Introduction	3 minutes
	Practice item	6 minutes (including output)
	Practice item	6 minutes (including output)
	Practice item	6 minutes (including output)
	Process discussion	8 minutes
	Principles	4 minutes
	Total	33 minutes

II	Introduction	3 minutes
	Practice item	6 minutes (including output)
	Process discussion and principles	10 minutes
	Practice item	7 minutes (including output)
	Practice item	7 minutes (including output)
	Total	33 minutes

DIFFICULTIES

Some of the difficulties that might arise with the lessons are outlined below. Teachers will of course have their own personal way of dealing with these difficulties, and with many teachers the difficulties may never arise. It is useful, however, to be able to anticipate them.

Sameness

Sometimes, at about the fourth or fifth lesson, students may start to complain that the lessons are too much alike. This tends to happen when the teacher has not focused attention on the process but has run each lesson as a general discussion on the content of the practice items. Clearly the content is rather similar since the range of problems is the same, **so unless the focus is on the process the lessons may well become too much alike.**

The students may also expect the lessons to be all fun and games. When they find that this is not so, they may be disappointed until they realize what the special purpose of the lessons is and start to enjoy them in their own right. There may thus be an awkward period around the fourth and fifth lesson, but when this is passed there is no more trouble.

Teachers are free to introduce as much variation as they wish. They may alter the format of the lessons or they may introduce variation into the ways the practice items are handled. This can be done in a number of ways, some of which are suggested in this book and others that teachers may invent for themselves. Devices like role-playing, play-acting, and getting the groups to criticize each other's output are only three of the possible variations.

With all these variations, the teacher must be conscious of two dangers and must avoid them. The first danger is that the lessons become general topic discussions. This may work very well at the time, but the development and transference of thinking skill as such may be very poor. The second danger is that there is so much playing around with the structure that the lessons become very disorganized and gimmicky. In both cases, the main purpose of the lessons is almost sure to be lost. Whatever variation is used, **the focus of the lesson must be on the thinking process that is the basis of the lesson.** As soon as a particular variation like play-acting becomes an end in itself it might be very enjoyable but the transfer value may be nil.

So what?

Sometimes, the students accept the lessons but cannot see the purpose behind them. Where this seems to be the case, the teacher should intersperse the lessons with test material so that the students can match their thinking in action. The teacher should also read the Perspective Section of this book and explain the purpose of the lessons. **But the main remedy is in the treatment of the ideas put forward.** If the teachers seem to be accepting everything that is offered then the students wonder how it can be worth anything. Teachers should be careful to avoid the impression that anything goes. They should differentiate between various responses praising some and criticizing others. They should maintain a tight control of the pace of the lessons, otherwise it can easily flop into the "so what?" mood.

The main point is that teachers should maintain the initiative both in the pace of the lessons and also in the way they treat the suggestions made. The students **do need** to be given a strong sense of achievement – not necessarily on a competitive basis but so that they feel they have actually achieved something. This sense of achievement is given by the way the teacher discriminates between different ideas. This is not easy and the basic rule is that if a person is really trying then condemning the idea will not help. Instead of condemnation the teacher should try to develop the idea until it does make sense. But if a person is not trying and thinks the idea is wonderful, the teacher should judge it objectively.

Underextended

At first sight, many of the practice items may seem rather easy. The items themselves are of course neither easy nor difficult. If they are tackled in a superficial way they will be easy but if they are tackled in depth they will be difficult. (The author has spent a lot of time teaching thinking to very sophisticated audiences and has never found that simple problems bored them.) The level of difficulty depends on the way the teacher presents the problem and especially with the sort of solution accepted. So, for students who feel that they are underextended, the teacher must demand a very high standard of response and must not be afraid of rejecting superficial approaches.

With many of the high-achieving groups there are complaints that individuals cannot show their excellence because it is submerged in the group output. This is not actually true since after the designated group has given its output, individuals in the other groups can add their own points. Nevertheless, it is useful from time to time to use the test material and also to get the individuals to operate on their own with an essay type output.

As before, **it is essential that teachers retain the initiative and keep a brisk pace.** Teachers should avoid being pinned down by individual controversies. The teacher has to make the rules of the game very clear to the students because this is what they expect. The students will want to know what achievement consists of in the lessons. Achievement is being able to carry out a particular thinking process deliberately, fluently and with precision.

Facetiousness

Facetiousness is not peculiar to the thinking lessons but may be encouraged by the group format. It may also be encouraged if the teacher tries to put a "game" atmosphere into the lesson or gives the impression that any idea will do. A facetious group can be split up. Facetious individuals need not be asked for their ideas. If facetiousness is a problem, then the emphasis on important ideas as opposed to trivial or silly ones can be brought into the lessons at an early stage.

BACKGROUND TO THE TEACHING OF THINKING

The idea of teaching thinking directly as a subject in its own right may seem very obvious. And so it should. However, there have been various approaches developed over time to teach thinking, most of which have been an outgrowth of the natural ability to think (commonly referred to as "the natural approach"). A comment on these methods is given below, followed by a detailed description of the essence of the **CoRT** method.

THE NATURAL APPROACH

"We don't need to learn thinking as a special subject because thinking is part of every subject. For instance in history we have to think what the teacher wants us to say."

The student who made the above statement was right. Thinking is part of every subject because it is part of life. It is as natural as walking or breathing and we do not really need to be taught these things. One of the most common objections to the direct teaching of thinking arises from the assumption that thinking is natural and needs no special attention. Everyone supposes themselves to be excellent thinkers and to perform as a matter of course the various thinking operations put forward in the thinking lessons.

The objection is difficult to disprove because one cannot easily convince people that they are not thinking the way they imagine themselves to be. The only way is to use experimental evidence. For example, most people claim that they are open-minded and always look at both the positive and negative aspects of a situation. However, on many occasions, the author has carried out a simple experiment in which people are asked to look at an idea which appears false at first sight. The ratio of negative to positive responses is consistently around 20:1. When the people are deliberately asked to make positive comments, they are able to do so. **Quite clearly, it is not natural to look for the positive aspects of something one does not like. A conscious effort is required.**

Two groups of 12-year-old students were asked to write an essay on the idea of weekend imprisonment for minor offenders. One group had completed the first thinking lesson (**PMI**, which concerns the examination of both positive and negative aspects of an idea), while the other group had not. The group which completed the lesson gave three times as many arguments **against** their final verdict than the other group. In other words, **the CoRT group was far more likely to see both sides of the idea.** The total number of arguments was also almost doubled.

The experimental results shown on pages 64-66 also indicate that **direct attention to thinking can have striking results.** Nevertheless, in spite of results like these, people will still maintain that thinking is natural and best left alone.

Running is also natural but an athlete can be coached to a much better performance. A natural performance may well be below potential. A natural performance may only be adequate to deal with a very familiar situation but inadequate for anything new. This certainly applies to thinking. Are we right in claiming that the natural ability to think is anywhere near the full potential?

We can now look at the various methods that have been used to try and improve upon the natural ability to think.

THE LOGIC APPROACH

Logic is sometimes taught as a subject in its own right. There is no doubt that it is a valid subject, but it is limited in its usefulness for teaching the general subject of thinking. Logic can tend to become an abstract semi-mathematical game in itself. A person may learn all the rules but find it impossible to apply them in real life situations where most of the thinking takes place during perception.

The old emphasis of logic was on syllogistic structures, and although this has an obvious usefulness in argument, it is only a tiny part of practical thinking. Excellence in logic does not help with making decisions, planning, guessing, defining objectives, etc. The modern emphasis treats logic as a pure system allied more to computer science than everyday living. There are many practical aspects of thinking which are impossible to fit under the Logic subject heading. To be fair, the subject never claimed to deal with practical thinking.

BY-PRODUCT

The traditional view is that the ability to think is developed as a by-product of using the mind to learn such subjects as the classics, science, mathematics, history etc. It is true that in these various subjects students do have to use their thinking. The amount of thinking they have to do varies very much with who is teaching the subject. But the thinking is all of a certain type – analytical, critical and organizing. For instance, in science the emphasis is on collecting facts before reaching a conclusion, whereas in real life a practical decision may be called for when there are few facts at hand. It is probably true that a very gifted and determined teacher can use any subject as a basis for teaching thinking, but this remains a cumbersome and inefficient way of doing it. In most subjects the sheer knowledge content of the subject makes it easy for the student to substitute this knowledge base for thinking. **It is very difficult to focus on process if content can by itself determine the line of thought.**

DISCUSSION

There is a growing tendency towards open-ended discussion subjects which come under such headings as General Studies, Liberal Arts, Social Studies, Humanities, etc. Such topics as the environment, drugs, population, traffic, and interpersonal behavior are discussed directly or in connection with the film-strip or other resources. This approach is valuable because it encourages interest, awareness and fluency. It allows students to have their own ideas and develop confidence in expressing them. But the format is not in itself adequate for teaching thinking as a skill. Inevitably, the emphasis is on the content and on people's ideas about the content. It is more like a debate than a thinking lesson, and debates are not especially good at teaching people to think, since the skills involved are rather specialized. Furthermore, general attitudes are notoriously difficult to communicate.

PUZZLES AND GAMES

These can be extremely useful for illustrating points and for making thinking visible. They can also be useful for reducing attitudes that obstruct thinking and also for building up useful attitudes. The author very often uses puzzles and games for this purpose. Puzzles are much less useful than games because the skill is very difficult to transfer. Games or situations which require a repetition of the same thinking process can certainly develop useful thinking skills, but by themselves they are not enough. Their main purpose is to make the student conscious of thinking as a process and of some of the different types of thinking.

CoRT
THINKING

CRYSTALLIZATION

The essence of the **CoRT** Thinking Method is to focus attention directly on different aspects of thinking and to crystallize these aspects into definite concepts and tools that can be used deliberately.

A person in a dark room stumbles over the furniture. As the light improves, definite items of furniture become visible. It is now easier for this person to move around and make use of the furniture. The crystallization of certain aspects of the amorphous process of thinking into definite concepts is a similar process – but an intentional one.

So the general open-minded attitude that involves looking at all aspects of an idea is crystallized into the **PMI**. With the **PMI**, a student learns to look for the Plus, Minus and Interesting aspects of any idea presented to him or her. The general open-minded attitude is not easy to teach, not easy to learn and not easy to transfer. But doing a **PMI** is very easy.

Similarly most people believe that they look at all the consequences of an action or a decision but in practice this is rarely the case. To persuade them to look at consequences is at best a lengthy business. To teach them to do a **C&S** is much easier because a general attitude can now be treated as a definite operation.

Most of thinking takes place in the perception stage and is therefore a matter of directing attention. You cannot direct attention to a general attitude no matter how valuable, but you can direct attention to a specific concept/operation and this is even easier if it is converted into an actual tool. **The purpose of crystallization is two-fold. The first purpose is to allow students to look directly at a process as a deliberate tool instead of having to look only at content. The second is to allow them to use process as a deliberate tool.**

TOOLS, NOT ANALYSIS

The crystallization of different aspects of thinking into definite tools does not follow an analysis of thinking into its component parts. **The tools are related to the practical application of thinking, and it is this that is crystallized into a tool.** Thus the tools may at times overlap.

ARTIFICIAL

It is true that such labels as **PMI, C&S, CAF**, etc. are highly artificial. But this is deliberate. To crystallize a rather vague intention into a visible tool that can be used deliberately is artificial. If the labels were not artificial they would not work. Phrases like *"look at consequences"* or *"evaluate an idea in terms of positive, negative and interesting features"* are too general and too vague. They are also too cumbersome. It is necessary to have something crisp and definite. It is also necessary to have something new, otherwise people will pay no more attention to *"looking at consequences"* than they have always done.

Some teachers will find these devices rather awkward to use at first. But students do not seem to have this problem and they use the short-hand labels without self-consciousness.

STRUCTURE

Some people object to the idea of imposing any structure on thinking, for they feel it should be unconstrained and free. This consideration of structure is a very fundamental one. It is absolutely essential to distinguish between two sorts of structure. One sort of structure is imprisoning. Being confined to a room, being trapped in a channel, being expected to follow a certain routine are all examples of restricting structures. But a lawn-mower, a hammer, a cup, a ladder and notation are all examples of liberating structures. They are tools which we can use when we want to. They are tools which make it easier for us to do certain things. It is a mistake to regard all structure as confining. Some structures are very liberating in the sense that we can do more *with* them than we could have done *without* them.

ARRIVING AT THE SECOND STAGE

The first stage is the deliberate recognition and use of the artificial tools. As skill develops in the use of tools, they can be used in different situations. The deliberate use of the tool always carries with it the attitude behind its use. In time, the attitudes themselves become the tool and the actual tool can drop away. In fact when children who have had the thinking lessons tackle actual situations they find themselves using the tools without having to mention them by name. The artificial labels act as a carrier or package. You may need a package to carry food around but you do not eat the package. It is this second stage – **habitual and confident use of the various thinking operations** – that is of course the aim. But the deliberate crystallization stage is a necessary one. Without it, everything stays in the realm of well-meaning, vague, undefined and unusable intention.

CONVENIENCE

Quite apart from the theoretical reasons for crystallizing various thinking operations into deliberate tools, there are simple reasons of convenience. Labels such as **PMI, CAF,** etc., can be used quickly and without cumbersome elaborations.

SUMMARY

Three basic methods can be used for finding one's way around a strange town.

1. Learn to use the fixed and predictable routes of buses, subways, trains, etc.

2. Get to know the town street by street until you can find your way anywhere.

3. Develop some general-purpose habits like buying a map, asking directions, getting taxis, finding your way to the main shopping area, etc.

The first method is what is called **the algorithmic method**: using pre-set and reliable routes for arriving at a solution. It is, of course, the basis of mathematical procedures. The second method is **the content method**: acquiring piece by piece as much knowledge about the situation as you can. (It is the basis of most of our subject teaching in education – for instance history, geography, science, etc.) The third method is **the general operations method** and is the one used by **CoRT** in its teaching of thinking. The general operations do not solve the problem but make it progressively easier to solve. **The general operations** have the advantage that **they are transferable** to any new town, whereas the content method is not transferable at all and the algorithmic method may or may not fit a particular situation.

EXPERIMENTAL RESULTS

On this and the next page are shown some results of the use of **CoRT** Thinking Lessons. In the first example 10 lessons had been done, and in the second example only one lesson had been done.

EXPERIMENT 1:

Tape recorded discussions by eight separate groups of elementary school students.

Of these eight groups four had done ten **CoRT** Thinking Lessons and the other four had not done any. The order of the groups was determined by tossing a coin.

Problem: A student wants to study to be a teacher. The student's parents have to live in another country for five years due to work. Should the student accompany them or stay with relatives or friends until the course is completed? (The school has many students whose parents work for the military; therefore, the problem is relevant to them.)

The following points were extracted from the tape by a researcher who had no idea which groups were which.

Points Considered	1	2	3	4	5	6	7	8
Language	X	X			X	X		X
Student's likes and dislikes (food, etc)		X		(X)				
Opportunities abroad or at home	X	X	X	X	X	X		X
Parents' attitude	X	X			X	X	X	
Practical difficulties abroad		X			X	X		
Practical difficulties at home				X				
Student's age and maturity			X					X
Climate		X	X	X	X			
Cost of living alone and studying	X	X			X	X		X
Would parents have a home abroad	X	X				X		
Other members of the family								
Cost of going abroad		X			X			
Keeping in touch with parents	X				X	X	(X)	X
Teaching-career prospects	X	X			X	X		
Training prospects	X				X			
Having congenial friends					X		X	
Vacations with parents	X	X			X	X	X	
Return to study after short stay	X	X	X		X			
Go abroad after study		X			X		X	
Father go abroad alone	X							
Teach (and study) abroad					X			
Parents visit on holidays						X		

Points Considered	Groups							
	1	2	3	4	5	6	7	8
Lose contact with friends		X				X		
Employment difficulties	X	X			X			
Opportunity to learn new language	X	X			X	X		
Opportunity to meet new friends		X						
Unsettling effect of changing jobs	X				X			
Parents' anxiety	X			X				
Anxiety about parents	X							
Risk of exam failure					X			
Able to support parents on return	X							
Able to maintain family home		X						
Totals	17	17	3	5	19	13	5	5
	(E)	(E)			(E)	(E)		

E=Experimental Group

EXPERIMENT 2:

Essay by two classes of 32 students each at a high school.

One of the classes had the first **CoRT** thinking lesson (on the treatment of ideas) and the other class had not.

Subject for consideration: "Do you think there should be special weekend prisons for minor offenders?"

	Class A	Class B
Total number for arguments put forward	200.0	105.0
arguments for	81.0	47.0
arguments against	119.0	56.0
Average number of arguments per person	6.2	3.3
Total number of different arguments	67.0	36.0
arguments for	31.0	17.0
arguments against	36.0	19.0
Arguments against a student's declared verdict as a percentage of arguments for that verdict*	58.7%	20.5%

Since 1978 John Edwards and Richard Baldauf, from the School of Education at James Cook University in Townsville, Queensland, Australia have conducted a series of research studies to look closely at the effect of **CoRT** in school settings.

Edwards and Baldauf (1983) report the introduction of **CoRT 1** into four grade ten (approximately 15 year olds) school classrooms. In a pre-post-test analysis of performance of both familiar and unfamiliar essay topics, the students showed statistically significant improvement. More interesting, a statistically significant relationship was found between **CoRT** gain scores and performance at the end of the year school exams, even when the results were controlled for the effect of IQ.

Edwards and Baldauf (1986 in press) looked in greater detail at the effects of **CoRT 1** on grade seven (approximately 12 year old students). They report strong anecdotal evidence from parents and students supporting the value of **CoRT 1.** The data also reveals statistically significant improvements in IQ, creativity (flexibility and originality) and self concept as a learner. In a very comprehensive study comparing 120 grade seven students studying **CoRT 1** with a control group of 80 students, again a range of effects was shown (Edwards and Baldauf, 1987 in press). The treatment students when compared with a control group

---

* In class A, 23 students put 80 arguments in support of their verdict and 47 against. In Class B, 28 students put 70 arguments in support of their verdict and 16 arguments against.

showed statistically significant improvement in IQ, as measured by the "Otis-Lennon School Ability Test, intermediate form R," overall academic achievement as measured by normal classroom tests with particular improvement in the language arts areas, originality as measured by the Torrance Test of Creative Thinking. The results also revealed large positive shifts in thinking approaches, flexibility of thinking and fluency. An interesting aspect of this study was the use of the Myers-Briggs type indicator to investigate the effect of, and on, student personality. The treatment studies showed relative shifts toward the more extroverted, more intuitive, and more judging (that is, more decisive and planned); of these only the shift towards extroversion was statistically significant. The use of Ryans' classroom observation record enables the effect of teaching **CoRT 1** on the characteristics of teachers to be investigated. Results showed marked improvement in the performance of some teachers – particularly in the areas of the more broad than narrow, more stimulating than dull, more original than stereotyped, and more adaptable than inflexible. These improvements were maintained after **CoRT** teaching had finished. All the above effects were obtained after only seven and a half hours of teaching **CoRT** thinking by untrained teachers.

References

Edwards J., and Baldauf R. B. Jr., "Teaching Thinking in Secondary School" in W. Maxwell (Ed) title *Thinking: The Expanding Frontier*. Philadelphia, Franklin Institute Press, 1983 pages 129-138.

Edwards J., and Baldauf R. B. Jr., "The Effects of **CoRT 1.** Thinking Skills Program on Students" in Bishop J., Lockhead, J and Perkins D. N. eds., *Thinking Progress in Research and Teaching*. Hillsdale, N. J. Erlbaum, 1986 (in press).

Edwards J., and Baldauf R. B. Jr., *"A Detailed Analysis of* **CoRT 1.** *in Classroom Practice"*. Paper to be presented to the Third International Conference on Thinking, at the University of Hawaii, January 1987.

CoRT THINKING IN SCHOOLS

INTRODUCTION

The **CoRT** Thinking material has been tested over a wide range of student ages and ability. Since the material provides only a trigger and a framework for thinking practice, it **can** be used over this wide range. The responses will of course be different even though the material remains the same.

PERSPECTIVE

These notes are intended to provide a setting or perspective for the **CoRT** Thinking Lessons. This perspective may be useful for teachers to pass on to the class if they want to know the purpose of the lessons. Both inside and outside the classroom, students are apt to feel that thinking is the same as discussion. They are apt to confuse articulateness or having a point of view with thinking as a skill. They are also apt to feel that thinking should not be tackled directly but as a "gut" feeling about a situation. But neither general discussion nor "gut" feeling are substitutes for thinking. They do have a great value in their own right, but thinking skill is needed to make the most use of this value.

If teachers choose to explain the purpose and perspective of the thinking lessons, this can be done as a discussion or dialogue with the class. The first point to be considered is whether thinking is natural or something that must be taught. Obviously, some thinking is natural, otherwise people would never be able to cope with everyday situations. But what about the situations with which people are not familiar? For instance choosing a career is not a situation a student will be familiar with through everyday practice. **The purpose of developing thinking as a deliberate skill is to enable a person to apply this skill to new and unfamiliar situations which have to be faced.**

Walking is natural and so is running. But athletes train and practice quite deliberately so that they can use their full natural potential. Well-trained athletes will always beat untrained athletes of the same natural ability because their use of energy is more economic and they have more stamina. Similarly, the purpose of training in thinking is to make it more focused and more economic and to enable people to tackle problems they would not otherwise be able to tackle.

Soccer players spend hours of practicing kicking and passing a soccer ball to each other. However, kicking and passing a ball are fairly natural. The players practice these things so that they can do them accurately and without hesitation when the need arises. The deliberate practice of different aspects of thinking has the same purpose: so that when we need to use these aspects we can do so accurately and without hesitation.

Once you have learned how to swim or ski it all seems very easy. But in order to learn how to swim or how to ski you have to spend some time doing it deliberately. You have to practice your swimming strokes in an artificial manner. You have to practice your stops and turns on skis. In fact in the beginning you may have to practice things which seem very unnatural like leaning outwards on a corner when skiing or submerging your head during part of a swimming stroke. All this may seem boring and unnecessary at the time but the ultimate aim is to make these things second nature to you. Similarly, with the thinking lessons the ultimate aim is to make the procedure second nature to you, but first you have to go through the practice stage.

Tools

The first point has been to show that what seems to be natural can still be improved by direct practice and training. The second point is to show the need for dividing thinking into different operations which are given such artificial labels as **PMI, CAF, C&S**, etc. These labels **have to be looked at as convenience labels**. Instead of having to ask people to look at all the consequences of a situation, you can use the short-hand of asking them to do a **C&S**. In addition, dividing things up and giving them a name makes it easier to pay attention to different parts of a total situation. For instance everyone knows what a horse looks like but it is not easy to discuss a horse with someone unless you know how to pay attention to different parts of it. Otherwise, you can only talk about a big horse, a strong horse or a good-looking horse. If, however, you can pick out the withers, the fetlocks, the shoulders, etc., and pay direct attention to them, your knowledge of horses is going to increase. Similarly, thinking is a very general subject that covers many things. It is useful to be able to focus attention on different aspects in order to talk about them and pay attention to them more directly.

In tennis, you make strokes to hit the ball, but you have to practice individual strokes, not strokes in general. For instance, you might practice a backhand slice or a top-spin forehand drive. You might practice a lob, a smash, a first serve or a second serve, etc. As soon as you can distinguish the different strokes from the general intention to get the ball back over the net, then you can practice them directly and acquire skill in using them. In a similar way, people who cannot separate out the different aspects of thinking may feel that they are very good at it, but in practice they are only good at one particular aspect. They may be very good at critical thinking or problem solving but useless at decisions or making plans. **So the purpose of the artificial labels is to make it possible to practice the different "strokes" or operations of thinking directly. The labels thus become tools.**

Skill

Skill consists of being able to deal effectively with a variety of situations. A skilled wood worker can deal with any number of situations involving wood. Skill depends on being able to recognize the situation and knowing how to deal with it. The thinking lessons are designed to enable students to recognize situations that require a certain type of thinking operation and to use that operation effectively.

At this point, teachers can refer to the experimental work, an example of which is shown on pages 64–65. Teachers can also comment on the experiment in which students who had done the first thinking lesson were three times more able than others to see both sides of a question.

Aim

The ultimate aim of the thinking lessons is very similar to that of coaching in sports: **to make the basic operations of thinking second nature so that they are carried out automatically, smoothly, and without fuss or effort.** This requires defining the operations and practicing them deliberately, and that is exactly what the **CoRT** Thinking Lessons are about.

TEST MATERIAL

A section on test material begins on page 74. This material is **not** designed to test the ability of the students or to examine how well they have learned the subject. **It is designed to give students an opportunity to display their skill in thinking.** High-achieving students often feel that during the lessons they do not get enough opportunity to show their skill because the group nature of the lessons does not allow individual brilliance and also the time is so brief. The test material allows the students to get their teeth into a situation. It allows them an opportunity to test their own achievement as they see how easily they can tackle the situations presented.

The test material may also be used with those students who feel that they know all there is to know about thinking. Such students can be given the test material at the beginning of the course and their output can be commented on. It is all too easy to assume that your thinking is excellent until you are asked to demonstrate its excellence. Comments on the students' output will tend to be along the lines of **what has been left out** rather than what is right or wrong.

In general, the test material is used to tighten up and give purpose to the lessons for those students who require this. If this is not done then the lessons can be seen to be a game in which anything goes and it does not really matter what is said. The test material can serve to bring home to the students the serious nature of the lessons.

Teachers should not feel that, because the subject is open-ended, test material is inappropriate. The test material is an opportunity for students to flex their intellectual muscles (as is an essay).

The test material can also serve to introduce variety into the lessons. For instance, it can allow the exercise of critical assessment. This is by far the simplest type of thinking since it involves reacting to something put in front of you rather than generating something on your own. It is also the thinking operation that is most trained in other subject areas. There is therefore some point in allowing students an opportunity to exercise this skill during the thinking lessons. This is done with the test material. (The change from group output to individual output in the test material also provides some variety.)

From the various points listed above it can be seen that the test material will be most appropriate for the older age groups and especially for those students who are most achievement conscious. It can also be used with classes where the students are lazy or feel that they know all there to know about the subject. With younger classes or well motivated classes the test material need not be used.

CoRT USE FOR DIFFERENT AGES AND ABILITIES

There are some differences in the way the lessons are run with different classes. We can consider the following basic types of use:

>   Elementary School   (5–12 years)
>   Junior High School   (12–15 years)
>   High School   (15–18 years)
>   Remedial Groups

ELEMENTARY SCHOOL

The material has been used with students over the age of 8. At this level, the effectiveness of the lessons depends very much on the motivation and skill of the teacher. There is no doubt, however, that the lessons can be used successfully with these young students. The lessons are less self-running than at more senior levels. The teacher has to maintain the momentum and keep this going by encouragement and suggestion. On the other hand, the

CoRT THINKING IN SCHOOLS

motivation and interest of students in thinking is very high in this age group. They really do get involved in the business of having ideas. They are much less inhibited than older students and much less bound by competition and other structures.

The lessons should not be called games but should be treated with all seriousness. One very successful teacher calls the lessons "Thinking Groups." The group size should be about 4–6 per group. The teacher reads out loud, elaborates and explains the lesson material because there may be reading difficulties in some of the groups. Nevertheless, the students are each given their workcards to keep as usual.

A very important point is to use those practice items which are going to be of interest to the students. This is not always easy to predict with this age group, and the usual mistake is to underestimate their interest and give them only child-type problems. They can get very interested in adult problems as well as those related to their own immediate world. In addition, there may be considerable interest in the science fiction type of problem. Students of this age are often more interested in ideas as such than are older students who prefer the problems that relate more directly to their own world. It is important to choose "rich" items where the student can easily picture the situation no matter how fantastic. The items should never be minimal ones which require the student to work hard before picturing the situation.

With these age groups, the lessons can be taken quite slowly. For instance, a lesson may consist of only two practice items and a general discussion. The discussion on the thinking process involved need not be separated but may be interwoven with the practice items. At first, the principles section may be left out, but this can be added quite soon. If there is time, the project section is used as a group discussion item rather than as an essay. Initially, the students may spend all their time pursuing matters which are not very relevant and also mixing up the practice items. The teacher need not worry too much about this as one of the most striking effects of the lessons is to is **to train students to direct their thinking in a more focused manner**. Experiments in which students who have done some thinking lessons are compared to others who have not, show very clearly that the lessons provide a framework which enables students to stick more closely to a problem instead of rambling from one subject to another.

Students do not mind the use of labels (**PMI, C&S,** etc.) and the teacher should feel embarrassed about using them. Confusion is the main difficulty in learning, and the labels are there to prevent this.

Since natural interest tends to be high at the elementary level, there is not much point in condemning ideas which seem way-out or trivial. At this age, ideas as ideas have a value for students and to condemn ideas simply introduces inhibitions without helping in any way. The teacher should try and maintain a strong flow of ideas and pick out and emphasize those which seem especially good. The three most important points for the elementary teacher to remember are:

1. Keep a high level of interest through choice of item and also interaction with the students.

2. Keep in mind the purpose of the lesson and the thinking operation that is the subject of it.

3. Do not reject ideas.

JUNIOR HIGH SCHOOL

At this age, the pressure of examinations is not so great as it is later, and there is therefore an opportunity to provide some basic groundwork in thinking. **The important point is for the teacher to be deliberate and definite and to treat the subject in a serious manner.** If the students begin treating the subject seriously, they are more likely to benefit from the lessons. At this level, the teacher may not be able to rely on naturally high interest levels but must provide a definite structure which the students can see and can work within.

The pace of the lessons must be brisk and crisp rather than discursive and sloppy.

Teachers should be free with their encouragement and praise and seek to guide the lessons in this way. They must also be quick to tighten up any lesson if it shows signs of losing focus. At this level (unlike the elementary level), the teacher does **not** have to accept all ideas. Indeed if teachers do so the students may not know what they are supposed to be doing. Teachers can judge some ideas to be important, interesting, original, etc., and others feeble, trivial and irrelevant. It is not a matter of trying to force good thinking through criticism but of **giving very clear guidelines.**

With this age group the lessons can be run in the intended manner. Since the pace is to be brisk, it should be possible to cover all the practice items. The process discussion section and the principles should also be covered. Unless it is more than a single period, the project section should be left out but it could be used as an essay subject or in a similar way.

Each student is given his or her own set of workcards to keep. Nevertheless, teachers should read out the practice items and try to enrich these. Choice of items will depend upon the teachers' assessment of their own classes. The items may have to be more relevant to the students' own lives since the students, unlike elementary students, are not as interested in ideas for the sake of ideas. Indeed, it is in this age group that immediate relevance may be **most important.** Students do, however, live in worlds quite apart from their own lives. For instance, through the medium of TV, students are conscious of war, cops and robbers, and various other situations they may never actually meet. So the teachers' assessment of relevance must take into account not only the students' direct world but also the "second-hand world" derived from the media. Fantasy is not as wide ranging as with younger students but is focused on fairly well defined alternative worlds. Political and social realism problems are possibly less applicable at this stage than at either the younger or older age levels.

The teacher must also try to provide variety by altering the format of the lessons and allowing interaction between groups.

The important points for the teacher to remember at this age level are:

1. Keep the lessons serious, deliberate and definite rather than playing around.

2. Keep the lesson brisk and crisp.

3. Provide by example definite guidelines and objectives so that the students do not flounder.

4. Be quick to control facetiousness and laziness.

If teachers feel that the class needs tightening up because the students have too high an opinion of their thinking skills, they may wish to use some of the test material given later in this book.

HIGH SCHOOL

At this level, the material may be used in a number of ways. It may be used as part of Liberal Arts or General Studies programs. Some schools are using it as a core subject for Social Studies.

The use of the material in high school classes introduces problems that are not apparent in the other groups. At this stage, the students have already been exposed to several years of secondary education. They are used to definite subjects with a deliberate content and syllabus structures. They are used to individual achievement often on a competitive basis and are accustomed to being graded.

The most important point here is that the students **should know exactly why they are studying thinking.** They must not get the feeling that the subject is only a time filler. Nor should they feel that the subject is only an adjunct to liberal arts and is not regarded seriously by the school. The section on "perspective" in this book is especially applicable at this age.

Suggestions for teachers

The teacher must set the scene for the lessons and must conduct them in a very business-like manner. At this stage, students tend to be very achievement conscious. The teacher must therefore make it possible for the students to know what they are trying to achieve and to feel that they have achieved it when they have. **Ideas can therefore be judged much more critically than at other levels**. Indeed, if ideas are never judged, the students soon believe that they know all there is to know about thinking. For the same reason, test material can be used very frequently.

Because students are geared to individual effort and achievement, they should be given some tasks (for instance, the test material) to do on their own and not in groups. When groups are used in the actual lessons, students should also be allowed to respond as individuals and not only through the group output. **This always applies to the process discussion section and can also apply to the practice section during which individuals can add to the output of the designated group.**

Students may, from time to time, be encouraged to suggest their own problems and thinking situations. For instance, teachers could collect such items from each member of the class and feed back the ones that seemed most interesting. At this stage, the choice of practice items can include items relevant to the student's own immediate world, to the world they see around them, and also to more general social and political questions like environment, housing, politics, etc. Teachers can also require the class to tackle items which may not interest them directly. **This is important because it should be possible to apply the skill of thinking to any problem, not just the ones that interest you.**

Maintaining focus on the thinking process

With this group more than with any other group, there is a danger that the emphasis on the thinking process is lost as the students diverge into an interesting discussion on the content of one of the practice items. This is a very real danger and teachers must be able to prevent it. The lessons are not meant as topic discussions but as opportunities to develop thinking skill through directing attention to some aspect of the process. Teachers must re-emphasize the process under consideration and keep bringing the students back to this. They must not be afraid of using the labels (**PMI, C&S, AGO**, etc.). When the **CoRT** material is used as a core subject for Social Studies it is even more important to use these labels since the tools involved can then be applied more directly to the other subjects in the programs. The transfer effect is even more important in this case.

Because this age group is more articulate, wordiness can be a problem. Teachers can reduce this in several ways. They can ask students to summarize their points, they can suggest a written output in note form, or subdivide the larger problems into smaller ones. Instead of having each group tackling the same large problem, each may tackle some aspect of it. Test material and essay use of the project section can provide opportunities for students to write out their thoughts in full.

The lessons can be run as intended. The groups should be kept small, and if possible there should be no more than four students per group. Output from the groups is verbal but an output in written note form can be used more often. More time should be allowed for the process discussion and principles section than at other age levels, even if this means reducing the practice items to two. In the principles section students may be asked to put in a principle of their own in addition to commenting on those given. The project section should be used more freely in this group either during the lesson itself, if this is long enough, or else as an essay subject. During the lesson itself, critical comment from one group about the thinking of another group may be allowed.

In general, the teacher can demand much more from students in this age group. The practice items may seem simple but they are expected to be approached with sophistication and in depth. An answer that may have been very good at a younger age level may no longer be good enough at the high school level.

The most important points for teachers to keep in mind are as follows:

1. The students must know exactly what they are doing and why they are doing it.

2. Teachers must provide opportunities for the students to have a sense of achievement. (This includes use of the test material.)

3. Teachers must keep the emphasis on the thinking process being examined and must not allow the lesson to become a general topic discussion.

4. Teachers can expect a sophisticated treatment of the practice items.

In short, the students can be stretched, but they **must** know what they are trying to achieve.

REMEDIAL GROUPS

The structure of the lesson with these groups is rather different. The class must be small in size – about twelve is the limit. Instead of dividing into groups, the students sit in one group with the teacher in the center. The lesson can become a dicussion session on a practice item. The thinking process involved is woven into this discussion rather than treated separately. This also applies to the principles section, which is not treated separately and may even be left out.

Teachers may have to do a considerable amount of scene setting, prompting and questioning. Above all, they should be able to take a suggestion from a student and re-phrase it so that it makes sense to the rest of the group. Otherwise, good ideas that are badly expressed could get lost. The re-phrasing also provides a model for the students to clarify their own thinking. Teachers should also take the trouble to link different suggestions together: "That idea is connected with Jim's idea to . . ."; "Which of these two opposite ideas do you like best?"; "We now have two ways of doing this, one from Sally and one from Hector – can anyone think of a third?"

The main problem is distraction. Two students start a private conversation of their own. One student takes something that is mentioned casually and makes it a whole new line of thought. Personal anecdotes relating to the situation are very frequent. **The main task of the teacher is to provide a framework for the ideas which is what is most lacking.**

The lesson material is not used in the usual way. Teachers pick out one or two practice items and these form the backbone of the lesson. The lesson is run as a discussion. As suggested earlier the thinking process is woven into the discussion and there are not separate discussion and principles sections. The project section is not normally used but a project item can be given to the group to think about before the next session.

The important points for teachers are:

1. The teacher is the focus of the lesson and keeps things going by prompting, suggestions, questions, etc.

2. The teacher operates by encouragement rather than condemnation. In particular, the teacher re-phrases suggestions made in order to give them the full value they deserve.

3. Distraction is controlled by firm re-statement of the problem and bringing back into the discussion those who have strayed out of it.

4. The main aim of the teacher is to build up a framework for the thinking of the whole group.

TEST MATERIALS

The test material serves three purposes:

1. **Individual:** During the thinking lessons, the students work in groups and do not get much chance to work as individuals. The test material gives them this chance. It also gives them enough time to work over a problem more fully than is possible during the lessons.

2. **Achievement:** Some students are apt to believe that thinking is natural and that their own thinking is perfect. The test material provides an opportunity to see whether this is indeed the case. The material is a means of tightening up the lessons. Conversely, the test material provides an opportunity for students to demonstrate achievement and to practice the thinking skills they have learned during the lessons.

3. **Effectiveness:** The test material provides a means for teachers to assess the effectiveness of their own teaching.

WHEN TO USE TEST MATERIAL

There are two main uses of the test material:

1. **Interspersed:** With high-achieving students, older students, and students used to tightly structured subjects, the test material can be interspersed with the lessons. This is especially necessary when the lessons appear to lack purpose in the view of the students. Use of the test material after every third or fourth lesson would be appropriate.

2. **Experimental:** This is to test the effect of the lessons on the students. In this case, material usually would be used at the beginning of the course and again at the end. It could also be used at the beginning and then after a particular lesson.

HOW TO USE THE TEST MATERIAL

Time and place

In schools where it is customary to give students material to work on in their own time, the test material can be used in this way. Otherwise, one of the thinking lesson periods may be given over to the test material.

It is not advisable to try to tackle a full thinking lesson and also test material in the same period (unless it is a double period). The test material can also be used as essay material and therefore can serve a dual purpose. In this case, it would be administered in the usual way essays are administered.

Time allowed for the test material would vary from 15 minutes to 35 minutes depending on the nature of the item chosen.

Output

The student's test output is always written, otherwise it would be no different from the thinking lessons themselves. For this reason the material is not suitable for younger children or remedial groups. The written output can take two forms:

1. **Essay**: Students write down their thinking in essay form. Obviously students work as individuals.

2. **Notes**: Individuals or groups can put down their output in written note form.

Material

Test material can come from various sources. The project items in the lessons can be used for the essay type of test. Teachers may wish to make up their own problems. A further selection of problems is given below.

ESSAY TYPE

Below is a selection of items which can be used for the essay type test material. These are in addition to the unused project items from each lesson which can also be used. Should students inquire whether they are supposed to use a **PMI, CAF,** etc., they can be told to do as they think fit.

1. What do you think of the idea of having weekend prisons for minor offenders?

2. Should students be part of the rule-making process in schools?

3. What do you think of the idea that students should be paid a small wage for going to school?

4. There is a suggestion that when graduating from high schools, students should spend one year doing social work (e.g., helping old people, hospital work, cleaning up the environment). Do you think this is a good idea?

5. A boy is trying to decide between a career as a teacher or a law officer. How should he make his decision?

6. A grocery is losing so much money that the store owner may soon have to close the store. Why do you think the store is losing so much money?

7. It has been decided to teach students by television at home instead of having them attend schools. Do you think this is a good idea?

8. There is a new type of vacation in which you earn money in the morning and enjoy yourself the rest of the day. What is the purpose behind this idea, and what do you think would happen?

9. What would happen if young people, adults and old people had to abide by different laws?

10. Should people be subject to a dress code?

11. If about half the people dislike some law, can it still be a good law?

12. How often should rules be changed, and who should ask for them to be changed?

13. Gasoline rationing is introduced. Why do you think this might happen, and what would happen as a consequence?

14. What do you think of the idea that students should be able to leave school as soon as they can read and write?

15. Because of increasing mechanization, there comes a time when everyone retires at 40 so that there are enough jobs to go round. What effects will this have?

16. A new type of marriage that only lasts for three years is suggested. Is this a good idea?

17. Should a company making shoes change the style as often as it can?

18. What do you think are the objectives and priorities of people running TV companies?

19. A man is found to have stolen a large number of left shoes. What do you think he is up to?

20. An architect declares that he prefers to build ugly houses – why?

21. The government decides to raise the minimum age for dropping out of school to 18. Discuss this idea.

22. The police are given different colored hats to wear (red, blue, green, etc.). What is the point of this?

23. Someone tells you that someone else is saying nasty things about you. What should you do?

24. If you were in the government and had to raise money by taxation, which things would you choose to tax?

25. Would it be a good idea for political parties to choose women candidates rather than men?

26. A city council decides to remove all traffic lights in its city. Discuss this idea.

27. If you had to choose, which would you prefer: to be smart, to be hard-working, or to be well-liked?

28. If you wanted to make lots of money, how would you set about doing it?

29. If you were a parent, would you allow your children to smoke, and if not why not? What are the arguments on each side?

CRITICISM TYPE

In the essay type of material, the students are asked to generate ideas about a situation. In the criticism type, they react to ideas which someone else has generated. Some possible examples are given below. If teachers wish to generate further examples of their own, they should not try deliberately to include mistakes but should set down a piece of thinking and allow the students to point out the mistakes. Topical items can be used here.

"A medical school decides that since the world needs more doctors it would be better to make the medical course shorter and easier. This would mean that some of those who become doctors would not know as much as before, but this risk would have to be taken."

Criticize the thinking involved here.

"The school board agreed that there were some things which young people understand better than their elders. So they set up a body of young people to advise them. But these young people were invited from other schools because the school board did not want the students to make rules for themselves."

Criticize the thinking involved here.

"*A town council decided that traffic congestion was getting very bad and that it would cost too much to try to reverse it. So they remove all restrictions on parking and actually encouraged more cars to drive into the city. Their idea was that things would get impossible that people would soon stop trying to drive into the city.*"

Criticize the thinking involved here.

"*In order to reduce the cost of living, the government increased the tax on cigarettes and alcohol but introduced a subsidy for meat and bread.*"

Criticize the thinking involved here.

"*A company decided that research was too expensive. So instead of doing their own research they waited for other people to make new discoveries and then either borrowed the ideas or bought the company involved. This way other people took the risk.*"

Criticize the thinking involved here.

"*A principal decides that his students are not working hard enough, so he insists that each week the students must take a test. If the students in a class do badly in the test, then the whole week's work has to be repeated.*"

Criticize the thinking involved here.

"*A boy is confused over which girlfriend he really likes best, so he pretends to be bored with both of them. He reasons that if he does not see either of them he will soon be able tell which one he misses most.*"

Criticize the thinking involved here.

"*A girl leaving school has to choose a career so she writes down on a piece of paper all the things she likes. She then asks her parents to write down what they think she will be good at. She then sees how the two lists compare. Those items which occur on both lists she puts in a hat and draws one out.*"

Criticize the thinking involved here.

"*A doctor finds that he has too many patients to handle. He thinks this is because his patients are always bothering him with matters that are not very serious. So he invents a very bad-tasing medicine which he gives to everyone of his patients no matter what illness they have.*"

Criticize the thinking involved here.

"*A company makes a point of employing only people who are smart, but not the smartest. The company says that the smartest people are not used to working hard and will not take orders from someone less intelligent than them.*"

Criticize the thinking involved here.

"*Leaders of a certain union are about to make a wage increase demand. They know they will get all they ask for. They also know members of their union do not like strikes. So they ask for a very large wage increase – that way, if it comes to a strike there will be something big to strike about.*"

Criticize the thinking involved here.

"*Because newspapers find that bad news is more interesting than good, it is suggested that there should be a tax on bad news, so that only the bad news that was really important would be published. Then people would get less depressed.*"

Criticize the thinking involved here.

ASSESSMENT

What happens to the test material output? The teacher will want to make some sort of assessment which can be used as a basis for a class discussion. The main basis for such an assessment would be as follows:

1. Comprehensive: By looking through all the outputs, teachers can get a good idea of the important points. They may also have some of their own which no one had mentioned. The emphasis here is on whether the main points have been touched upon or left out.

2. Organization: Although a rigidly structured organization of ideas is not desired, the ideas should be presented in some sort of order and with clarity.

3. Interest: Sometimes, one student may bring up a point which though not a major point is novel and interesting. This is given credit so long as it is relevant.

4. Opinion: Teachers may disagree with various points raised. They should voice this disagreement (not to the extent of saying that the other point of view must be wrong, but by saying that they do not agree).

5. Thinking process: The deliberate or implied use of a particular thinking process can be commented on. Similarly, failure to use a process can also be commented upon. For instance, if someone fails to pay any attention to consequences, this can be noted. This sort of thing can be done by comparison between individual outputs or on a group basis.

EXPERIMENT

There are two main ways in which the test material can be used for experimental purposes in order to see what difference the lessons have made to the thinking of the students: control groups and crossover.

Control Groups

In schools where one class is doing the thinking lessons and a parallel class is not, then it is sometimes possible to give the same test items to the two groups and then compare the output. This can be done in the form of an essay. Naturally, the group which has done the thinking lessons should not be given any special instructions to remember them.

Crossover

Here the class serves as its own control group. One half of the class tackles test item A and the other half test item B. Later the two are reversed and the group that tackled item A now tackles item B. In this way the effect of the lessons on tackling both A and B can be seen since there are before and after results for each item. For instance, the first stage of the crossover can be done before any lessons are given and the second stage at the end of the term.

RESEARCH

The most important thing about the lessons is that they should be effective in developing thinking skill. Teachers who would like to pass their comments about these thinking lessons on to the author are invited to write to Dr. de Bono, c/o the Publisher.

The author wishes to emphasize that the teacher's comments need not be long, complex, or full of theory or jargon. Often the simplest observations turn out to be the most universal and therefore the most useful.

There are three main ways in which the teacher can help:

Observation:

In the course of running the lessons, the teacher cannot fail to notice certain things: how the students react, which lessons work best and which worst, the types of responses, difficulties, points which arouse most interest, the type of problem liked best or least. Observations may be of a general nature and apply to the atmosphere of the class or the general performance of the students. But observations can also be much more specific and be about individuals. For instance, one teacher noticed how a boy who was on the verge of being sent to a remedial group suddenly brightened up in the thinking lessons and became the leader and spokesperson of a group that contained the brightest students in the class.

Variation:

The teacher may decide to alter the way the lessons are run. These alterations may apply to the basic format or individual practice items. If these variations work, it would certainly be most useful to hear about them. There are, however, two dangers. This first is that the teacher tries alteration after alteration just for the sake of this. The whole thing can become very gimmicky and the students thoroughly confused. The second danger is when the variation results in a lesson which might be very interesting in itself but is only remotely connected with teaching thinking as a skill. This can easily happen with general discussion lessons, role-playing, debates, etc. The most useful sort of variation is when the teacher notices something that works particularly well during a lesson and then tries to introduce this deliberately as a variation.

Output:

Students' individual comments can be reported back to **CoRT**, as they are often very revealing. One school had its students do a **PMI** on the thinking lessons themselves and this was a very good idea. Written output either in note form or essay form from tests or from ordinary lessons can also be sent on to **CoRT**. So can tape-recorded discussions. Whether teachers use the test material and format suggestions in this book or devise their own, the results would be of great research interest. Results may not seem to be important to the person sending them, but when put together with results from other schools they may help complete the picture. No one should be timid about sending material, no matter how inadequate it may seem.